The State and Place of the Dead

WHAT HAPPENS AFTER WE DIE

by

W. Edward Bedore

The State and Place of the Dead

What Happens After We Die

by

W. Edward Bedore

BEREAN BIBLE INSTITUTE
116 Kettle Moraine Dr. S
PO Box 587
Slinger, WI 53086

Web: bereanbibleinstitute.org
E-mail: bbi@bereanbibleinstitute.org
Phone: 262.644.5504

The State and Place of the Dead
WHAT HAPPENS AFTER WE DIE

By W. Edward Bedore

Copyright © 2012 by Berean Bible Institute, Inc.
ISBN: 978-0-9853663-0-8

Second Printing 2015

BEREAN BIBLE INSTITUTE
116 Kettle Moraine Dr. S
PO Box 587
Slinger, WI 53086

Web: bereanbibleinstitute.org
E-mail: bbi@bereanbibleinstitute.org
Phone: 262.644.5504

All rights reserved. No part of this book may be reproduced in any form without permission in writing, except in the case of brief quotations in critical articles or reviews.

Printed in the United States of America

TOTAL PRINTING SYSTEMS
NEWTON, ILLINOIS

TABLE OF CONTENTS

CHAPTER 1 9

The Intermediate State

    The Rich Man & Lazarus
    Purpose of the Story
    Conscious State of the Dead
    Proofs of Personal Consciousness after Physical Death
    Practical Application

CHAPTER 2 31

Hell, Sheol, Hades, Paradise, and the Grave

    The Final Hell
    Sheol/Hades:The Present Hell
    Sheol is Not a Burial Place
    Hades Not a Place of Silence
    Death and Sheol
    Tartarus
    Paradise
    The Grave
    Other Arguments
    Practical Application

CHAPTER 3 63

The Resurrections and Judgments

    The Resurrections
    The Judgments
    The Nature of Judgment in the O.T

CHAPTER 4 71
Universalism and Annihilationism

   The Doctrine of Universalism
   An Important Consideration
   Universalism's Evidence
   Many Made Righteous
   Everlasting Lake of Fire
   Bowing of Every Knee
   The Kingdom and the Lake of Fire
   Thoughts Regarding Universalism
   The Doctrine of Annihilationism
   Man is Only Two Parts
   The Divine Satire Theory of Luke 16:19
   The Placement of the Comma in Luke 23:43
   Absent From the Body
   Paul's Desire to Depart and Be With Christ
   Wise Words From the Past

CHAPTER 5 121
Conclusion

APPENDIX 123
Further Considerations

   The Influence of Marvin Vincent
   The Use of Aion and Aionios in the Septuagint
   Aion is Used for Olam in the Septuagint
   Aionios is Used for Olam in the Septuagint
   Aion is Used in the Septuagint for Ad and Gad

Bibliography 139
Scripture Index 141

Dedication

This work is dedicated to those saints who, over the last 2,000 years, have dared to believe God and stand for the truths revealed in His Word. May their testimony serve as a challenge to the Body of Christ today to diligently defend and boldly proclaim the vital truths revealed in the Holy Scriptures.

1

The Intermediate State

The "intermediate state" is a term used in reference to the location and state of the human soul between the time of physical death and resurrection. There are two aspects to this state of being: one concerns saved individuals who look forward *"unto the resurrection of life"* and the other concerns the unsaved who will suffer *"the resurrection of condemnation"* (Jn. 5:28-29; cf. I Cor. 15:51-53; I Thes. 4:15-17; Rev. 20:4-6, 11-15).

THE RICH MAN & LAZARUS

Because of its importance to our understanding of what the Bible teaches about the intermediate state of the soul, the question is often asked, is the account of the Rich Man and Lazarus (Lk. 16:19-31) a historical account or is it a parable? Is it the true story of two men who lived and died during the time of Christ's earthly ministry, or is it a made-up story used by the Lord to drive home a point? I believe the evidence is that it describes an actual history of these two men and that, in the events described for us in this passage, we are given Scriptural proof of the continued conscious state of individuals after physical death. Because of the importance of this portion of Scripture as to what the Bible teaches about the State of the Dead, we want to look closely at it.

By definition a parable is a true-to-life story used to illustrate or illuminate a truth. This is true even if all of the details never occurred exactly as presented in the story. They are special stories that may, or may not, reflect historical events. Nevertheless, they must be true-to-life. By true-to-life we mean that a parable must be based on a real-life situation that the hearers are familiar with. In other words, the story itself has to be based on events that could have happened, whether they ever did or not.

Our English word "parable" is a transliteration of the Greek word *parabole*. It is a derivative of *paraballo*, which comes from two Greek words *para*, and *ballo*. *Para* means alongside or by the side of, and *ballo* means to lay, or to place, something. Thus, a parable is a story put down beside a truth in order to illustrate that truth through comparison. Therefore, a parable must be a true-to-life story in order for it to have any meaning to those who hear it. To try to use a fanciful story containing elements that have no basis to the world in which men and women live would only serve to confuse people rather than providing them with spiritual light.

A simple survey of the Lord Jesus' use of parables reveals that He always used things commonplace to daily life such as the building of houses, storing old and new wine, sowing seed, weeds growing along with the crop, yeast permeating bread dough, hidden treasure, fishing, monetary debts, unforgiveness, vineyards, family life, weddings, a barren fig tree, a lost coin, an unjust judge, etc. While His hearers may not have made the connection to the truths the Lord was pointing out, they needed no explanation as to what the stories were about because they involved common everyday things to which they could relate. When the hearers of the parables perceived that there was an analogy between the story and their own situation, they were prompted to think about it, hopefully to respond by faith to the truth illustrated. Parables can be extraordinary and even shocking, but never unrealistic or fanciful.

When we come to the account of the Rich Man and Lazarus, we find a situation different from what is found in any of the parables. The Lord Jesus' hearers could understand the contrast between the lives of a rich man and a poor beggar. It was common to see beggars sitting by the road hoping for a handout, and they could easily identify the folks who had more than enough wealth to live comfortably. Then, as now, there was a stark difference between the lives of those who had an overabundance and those with nothing. Although we can still grasp that there is a great difference between the lifestyles of these two men, the vastness of the "great gulf" between them is often lost to us because of the welfare and social services provided by the government. This is not the case in many third world nations today where people are literally starving to death. Regardless, the contrast in this story is the reversal of that gulf after the death of these two men.

The hearers of this story could follow the contrast between these two men right up to the moment of their deaths. At that point, however, the situation changed drastically. The outcome was something that they could not relate to any life situations that they had ever witnessed. The state and location of the departed soul was beyond their own life experiences, or what is commonly known to be true by the experience of others. The circumstances described go beyond the realm of the parable. That does not mean that it isn't a true-to-life story. Physical death is a natural part of the life experience of all mankind, but what takes place afterward is hidden from those who have not yet experienced it. In this account of a beggar and a rich man, the Lord was revealing the reality of what takes place following physical death to drive home an important truth. We should mention at this point that even if it was a parable, the place referred to as Abraham's Bosom and the account of what took place there would have to be based on reality for it to have any meaning.

Following are some reasons that this should be considered a history of two real men and not a parable.

> 1. Parables are true-to-life, but hypothetical, illustrative stories. The names of specific individuals are never given in them, but here the names of three men are given; Lazarus, Abraham, and Moses. Also mentioned are the "prophets" who were real people too. ("Moses and the prophets" is a general term for the whole Old

Testament that refers to its human authors). See below, use of personal names.

2. It does not have the normal form of a parable with an introduction, analogy story, and application. Instead, it is in the form of the narration of a real-life story given for the purpose of illustration.

3. It does not use the principle of comparison in a way that is characteristic of parables.

4. The discussion between the Rich Man and Abraham is not consistent with the parabolic style normally found in the Scriptures.

5. It seems obvious that in relating this particular story when He did, the Lord Jesus was using a real-life account that many of those listening to Him that day could readily relate to because they actually knew, or at least knew of, the two men involved. The rich man's brothers may have even been in the audience.

As we pointed out earlier "the names of specific individuals are never given in parables." Claiming that this is not so, the parable of the two sisters named Aholah and Aholibah (Eze. 23:1-4ff.) has been offered as proof that individuals are named in a Bible parable after all. However, when we look at the parable, we find that these are not the names of individuals at all but names with allegorical meaning that were assigned to the capital cities of Israel and Judah. Samaria in northern Israel was called "Aholah" and Jerusalem in southern Judah was called "Aholibah." Respectively, these names meant "her own tabernacle" and "My tabernacle is in her." This referred to the fact that unfaithful Israel had built a pagan temple to worship in, thus committing spiritual harlotry. Judah, on the other hand, had God's Temple in its capital of Jerusalem but still reverted back to idolatry and was thus worthy of the same judgment her sister to the north had already suffered. These names do not identify individuals, but refer to nations. Therefore their use in this parable does not disprove the statement that "in no parable is an individual named." [Luke 16:19-31 is not an exception to the rule, it is a narrative about real people and actual events.]

THE PURPOSE OF THE STORY

The main point of the story of the Rich Man and Lazarus is that an individual's wealth and social standing, or the lack thereof, is not necessarily an indication of that person's spiritual standing before God. Many of the Jews believed that the fact that they had accumulated wealth that afforded them social status and prominent positions in the religious community proved that they were under the blessing of God. They also thought, according to their logic, that those who were poor were under the curse of God. They no doubt appealed to the promises made to Israel in the Law of Moses concerning the blessings of prosperity for obedience to God's Law and the curses of poverty because of disobedience, failing to recognize that those promises were national in nature rather than personal (see Deut. 28:1-45 ff.; etc.).

They were also ignoring the many warnings found in *"Moses and the Prophets"* that were directed towards the leaders of Israel who selfishly misused their power and wealth (see Isa. 56:10-12; Ezek. 34:1-4 ff.; Micah 3:1-4; etc.).

To challenge their seriously flawed thinking, the Lord Jesus told the parable of the unjust (or dishonest) steward (Lk. 16:1-13). The main point of this parable was that the dishonest steward, who represented the Gentiles, was wiser than the *"children of light,"* a reference to the sons of Israel, who were to be a channel through which God's light would reach the Gentiles, i.e., the nations of the world (Isa. 42:5-7; 49:5-6; 60:1-3; 62:1-3). The true Light of the World is Jesus Christ Himself (Jn. 8:12), Who is the Messiah of Israel. In the Prophetic Program, the only avenue through which the Gentiles can come to the Light is through the Nation of Israel (Isa. 60:1-3; Zech. 8:20-23). The point of this parable was that those who were striving after riches were actually self-serving rather than servants of God. He was calling on them to choose between the two, saying: *"No servant can serve two masters: for either he will hate the one, and love the other; or else he will hold to the one, and despise the other. Ye cannot serve God and mammon* (money)" (Lk. 16:13). The implication was that those whose priorities were based on accumulating wealth were demonstrating that their hearts were not right with God (cf. Mat. 6:19-21).

On hearing Him, the Pharisees, who were lovers of money, scoffed at the Lord (Lk. 16:14), who then accused them of being self-righteous and trying to press, or force, their way into the Kingdom on their own terms (Lk. 16:15-16). That is to say, they were counting on their self-proclaimed righteousness to open the door of the Kingdom to them. Jesus plainly declared that the terms of the Law were solid and could not be circumvented. The principles underlying the Mosaic Law express God's character and, therefore, the Law is more enduring than the whole of creation (Lk. 16:17). He then revealed their hypocrisy by pointing out that their attitude about divorce and remarriage was not in line with God's purposes (Lk. 16:18; cf. Mat. 5:31-32; 19:3-9).

The key to understanding the point that the Lord is making in telling the story of the Rich Man and Lazarus is found in verses 15 and 16. *"And He said unto them, ye are they which justify yourselves before men; but God knoweth your hearts: for that which is highly esteemed among men is an abomination in the sight of God. The Law and the Prophets were until John: since that time the Kingdom of God is preached and every man presseth into it"* (Lk. 16:15-16).

Though their self-justification might gain them favor among men, it would not gain God's favor because He knew what was in their hearts (cf. Jer. 17:9-10). The things that men hold in high regard, things that gain them position and respect among men, are disgusting to God. In truth, the love of money reveals a covetous heart that has given its allegiance to "mammon" rather than God (cf. I Tim 6:10).

In the Law and the Prophets, a general term for the Old Testament Scriptures, is found the promise, or proclamation, of God's coming Kingdom on earth, which Israel was waiting for. John the Baptist came on the scene to introduce the Messiah, who would usher in the Kingdom Age, to Israel (Jn. 1:26-34). After being baptized by John, Jesus Christ began His public ministry by saying, *"The Kingdom of God is at hand: repent ye, and believe the Gospel"* (see Mk. 1:9-15).

Of course, the Jews, especially the Pharisees, knew that entrance into the Kingdom was conditioned on obedience to God's Law. To drive home His point about how the money-loving Pharisees were misusing their wealth to their own peril, the Lord told the true story of the Rich Man and Lazarus. The Rich Man wasn't lost because he had wealth, nor was Lazarus saved because he was poor. This was a matter of the heart with the focus being on the Rich Man, not Lazarus.

The Rich Man's failure to help Lazarus, a fellow Israelite, revealed that he had a wicked and non-repentant heart. By refusing to provide for the poor beggar sitting at his gate, the Rich Man was rebelling against God who, through Moses, had given Israel specific instructions on how those with resources were to treat their poor fellow countrymen (see Deut. 15:7-11). They were to open their hands wide in providing for the poor and needy in their land. This man showed that he did not love the Lord God of Israel with all of his heart, soul, and might as commanded by the Law (Deut. 6:4-5; cf. Mk. 12:28-30). The evidence of this was that he did not love his neighbor who in this case was Lazarus (Lev. 19:18; cf. Mat. 22:34-40). Although he thought he could force his way into God's Kingdom, his heart attitude, which was demonstrated by his actions, proved him to be unworthy to enter.

When he asked Abraham to send Lazarus back to warn his brothers about what awaited them beyond death's door if they did not repent, *"Abraham saith unto Him, 'They have Moses and the Prophets; let them hear them'"* (Lk. 16:29). If, like the Rich Man, his brothers would not heed the warnings found in God's Word from Moses and the Prophets, neither would they believe someone who had been raised from the dead. This proved to be true as even after His own resurrection the leaders of Israel rejected the Lord Jesus as their Messiah. It is sad to say but, for the most part, mankind has continued to reject the resurrected Christ as Savior even until today.

Being true-to-life, whether it is historical or parable, this story is based on truths from which we can learn certain facts about the state of those who have experienced physical death. This is true even though teaching these things was not the main purpose the Lord had in telling it. Being based on truth, the facts

The Intermediate State

learned from the experience of the Rich Man and Lazarus are consistent with what is found in other places in Scriptures. From this passage we know that:

1. After physical death, individuals continue to exist in a state of personal consciousness (vv. 22-25ff.; cf. Rev. 6:9-10).

2. Having experienced physical death, the individual's destiny is sealed. There is no opportunity to cross over from the place of utter hopelessness to a place of hope after physical death (vv. 25-26).

3. Hades is not a figure of speech but a real place of suffering to which the unsaved go to await the final judgment (vv. 23-24). They will stay there until the time of the resurrection to condemnation when they will be consigned to the Lake of Fire forever (cf. Rev. 20:11-15).

4. There is a place, referred to here as Abraham's Bosom, which is a place of comfort and joy (v. 25). The saved go there until the time of their resurrection unto life. This place is also referred to as "Paradise" in the Scriptures (cf. Lk. 23:39-43). Originally it was a partitioned section of Hades but was moved to heaven after Christ's resurrection. Paul speaks of being "caught up into paradise" (II Cor. 12:4). This implies that Grace saints and Kingdom saints may jointly occupy Paradise until the time of their respective resurrections.

5. After physical death, unsaved individuals will have regretful memories of the past and knowledge of their hopeless future (vv. 25-28).

6. After having died, individuals go to Hades or Paradise and are not able to return or send back messages to those who are still living (vv. 26-28). Samuel, Moses, and

THE STATE AND PLACE OF THE DEAD

Elijah are exceptions, having been sent by God as special envoys. No one can return by an act of their own will or be enabled to return from beyond the grave by mediums, channelers, etc. who summon them. The Scriptures leave no possibility for reincarnation and spiritism.

7. Neither the saved nor the lost will ever cease to exist, nor will they exist without form between physical death and the resurrection. Both have a temporary form of some kind that enables them to see, speak, hear and feel (vv. 22-25). While this form is of a spiritual nature and substance, it is still a tangible form with a recognizable human likeness.

THE CONSCIOUS STATE OF THE DEAD

The story of the Rich Man and Lazarus clearly shows that, after physical death, they were very much aware of their circumstances and what was going on around them. The Apostle Paul stated that for the believer *"to live is Christ, and to die is gain"* (see Phil. 1:21-23), indicating that this is in fact the case. That he had *"a desire to depart* (this life)" to be with the Lord tells us that he expected to consciously experience something *"far better"* than can be found in this life. This means that at the time of physical death believers will *"gain"* something. As precious as the believer's life is *"in Christ"* in the here and now, it will be greatly enhanced when he leaves it to enter into the presence of the Lord. Paul's statement that *"to live is Christ"* speaks of a purposeful life lived in service to and for the glory of the Lord Jesus Christ. The only way to add to this, to *"gain"* that which is better, is to enter into the very presence of Christ in heaven, to consciously enjoy perfect fellowship with Him in a way that we cannot in this life. It is only by faith that the believer can find the confidence to face death, *"willing rather to be absent from the body, and to be present with the Lord"* (see II Cor. 5:7-8).

That the death of a believer brings him, or her, into a situation considered to be *"gain,"* or the increased experience of spiritual blessing, refutes all erroneous ideas such as soul sleep or that the soul ceases to exist at death to be awakened or recreated at the time of the resurrection. To enjoy the life of Christ in this life, only to be experientially separated from Him by becoming unconscious or ceasing to exist would be loss, not gain. This would be true even if it was only for a short time. But the fact that we have been given eternal life guarantees that we have everlasting fellowship with God. Our life in Christ will never be diminished, only enlarged. That *"the love of God is shed abroad in our hearts by the Holy Spirit who is given unto us"* (Rom. 5:5) mandates the continued conscious existence of the believer after physical death because nothing, not even death, *"shall be able to separate us from the love of God, which is in Christ Jesus our Lord"* (Rom. 8:39).

SCRIPTURAL PROOFS OF THE CONTINUED PERSONAL CONSCIOUSNESS AFTER PHYSICAL DEATH

The Old Testament saints are pictured as being *"gathered to their people"* **after physical death**

(see Gen. 25:8; 35:29; 49:29,33; Num. 20:24,26; 27:13; 31:2; Deut. 32:48-50): To be gathered together with other people makes no sense, and has no meaning, if it only refers to entering into an unconscious state of being of some kind. To be gathered to their people speaks of being joined together in a relational way. In a prophecy about Josiah, given through Huldah the prophetess, a distinction between the king being gathered to his fathers and his body going to the grave is evident (see II Chron. 34:28).

His child having died, David expected to eventually go to his son (see II Sam. 12:13-23): If he had expected to enter into an unconscious state, he would have had no such hope. David fully expected to see his son on the other side of the vale of physical death. David's words, *"I shall go to him, but he shall not return to me,"* show that he did not have the hope of resurrection in mind, but to join his son after he died. Together they would await the resurrection while enjoying each other's company.

Samuel's appearance to Saul and the woman of Endor (see I Sam. 28:3-20): King Saul was struck with fear over a coming battle with the Philistines, and the Lord God was ignoring his petitions for guidance. He became so frightened and distressed that he sought out a necromancer in a desperate effort to contact Samuel, the departed prophet who had in better times been his spiritual counselor. It was a frightful shock to this woman when God allowed Samuel to actually appear

The Intermediate State

to deliver a prophetic message from the Lord to Saul. No doubt she either planned to trick Saul or expected a demon masquerading as Samuel to appear. Adding to her fear was the realization that the man who had come to her in an effort to communicate with Samuel was actually King Saul, who had a reputation for putting mediums like her to death. In his appearance, Samuel had a recognizable human form and was able to carry on a conversation with Saul. His complaint about being *"disquieted"* (disturbed) indicates that he was abiding in a state of conscious bliss that was interrupted in order for him to make this appearance. That it is said he was brought "up" rather then brought "back" shows that he was residing in the lower parts of the earth. We believe that he was in Abraham's Bosom, or Paradise, which at that time was located in the heart of the earth in a place called Sheol, or Hades (see below "The Repentant Thief on the Cross").

The Calling of Lazarus from the Grave (Jn. 11:1-46): Although the "how" is beyond our understanding, the fact that Lazarus responded to the Lord Jesus Christ's command to "come forth" from the grave speaks to us of the continued conscious existence of the soul following physical death. (This is not the Lazarus of Luke 16).

The Repentant Thief on the Cross (Lk. 23:32-34, 39-43): As they hung on their respective crosses, one of the thieves who was crucified with Christ turned to Him with a repentant heart saying, *"Lord, remember me* *when thou comest into thy kingdom."* Christ's response was to say, *"Verily I say unto thee, Today shalt thou be with me in Paradise"* (see Lk. 23:39-43). We know that at the time of His death the Lord Jesus descended to the *"heart of the earth"* where He stayed for three days and three nights Mat. 12:40) *"and preached to the spirits in prison"* (I Pet. 3:19). This tells us that up to the time of Christ's sacrifice for the sins of the world, *"Paradise"* was in the heart of the earth. He promised the repentant thief they would be together in Paradise that very day. This is the same place that is referred to as Abraham's Bosom in Luke 16:22. From II Corinthians we know that Paradise is now located in *"the third heaven"* (see II Cor. 12:1-4). Obviously, this abode of the saved dead was moved from the innermost parts, or the heart, of the earth to the heavenly abode of God. Paradise is the place where the souls of the redeemed reside awaiting the resurrection. Before the price of their redemption was paid on the Cross, it was located in the heart of the earth. But, after the full payment was made, it was relocated to the third heaven, or the Heaven of heavens, where God is. There they wait in God's presence for the time of their resurrection. The souls of all of the redeemed who have died since Jesus Christ's resurrection have entered into God's presence there, as to be *"absent from the body"* is to be *"present with the Lord"* (see II Cor. 5:6-8).

Jesus Christ's Direct Teaching that Departed Saints are Alive (see Mat. 22:23-32): Using a hypothetical situation, the Sadducees challenged the Lord Jesus concerning the resurrection of the dead, which was something that they did not believe in. The Lord turned the tables on them, though, by exposing their ignorance about the subject. First, He explained that in the resurrection, marriage would not be a consideration. He then went on to confront them on an important issue concerning the saints who have experienced physical death. He knew that the Sadducees not only denied a literal resurrection of the dead, but even denied the continued existence of the person after death. To reveal their error, the Lord quoted God's words to Moses at the burning bush, *"I am the God of thy father, the God of Abraham, the God of Isaac, and the God of Jacob"* (Ex. 3:6). Although Abraham, Isaac, and Jacob had died hundreds of years before the time of Moses, God used the present tense *"I am"* rather than the past tense "I was" when identifying Himself to Moses as their God. This shows that they were existing in a conscious state at that time. The Lord Jesus' remark, in the present tense, that *"God is not the God of the dead, but of the living"* (Mat. 22:32) reveals that they were still alive as He spoke, some 1500 years later. Being alive indicates a continued conscious existence. If this was true before the Cross, it is undoubtedly true of believers on this side of the Cross.

The Appearance of Moses and Elijah on the Mount of Transfiguration (Lk. 9:28-36): It could be argued that Elijah shouldn't be held up as an example because, rather then going through the normal experience of physical death, he was caught up into heaven in an unusual way (II Kin. 2:11). However, even though it was under unique circumstances, there is no doubt that Moses suffered physical death and his body was buried (Deut. 34:5-6). Moses, with Elijah, appeared on the mountain after Jesus Christ was temporarily glorified before the eyes of Peter, John, and James. They appeared in a recognizable form, and it is specifically stated that they spoke with the Lord about His impending death. This event reveals the continued conscious awareness of those who have departed this life. That Moses and Elijah spoke with Christ about His departure, which was about to take place at Jerusalem, confirms their continued ability to think, remember, and communicate. We don't have a record of exactly what Moses and Elijah spoke to the Lord Jesus about concerning the death He would die, but there can be little doubt that their conversation centered on what would be accomplished through the sacrifice of Himself for the sins of the world. He would fulfill the prophecies about Himself found in Moses and the Prophets (cf. Lk. 24:25-26, 44-48).

That Jesus Christ Will Bring the Departed Grace Believers with Him from Heaven at the Time of the Rapture of the Church (I Thes. 4:13-18): Those who have died physically are presently in heaven as their body "sleeps" in the grave. Returning with Christ from heaven (v. 14) when He comes for His Church, they will receive their glorified bodies first (vv. 15-16) and then those still living will receive theirs as they are caught

The Intermediate State

up to be with the Lord (v. 17; cf. I Cor. 15:51-54). That Christ will bring them from heaven with Him can only mean that they are first in heaven with Him.

The Martyred Saints of the Tribulation (Rev. 6:9-11; 7:9-10,14; 15:2): While the believers who will die for their faith in Christ during the Tribulation are particularly singled out here, it must be remembered that their status is that of Kingdom saints. That is to say that their hope is to enter into Christ's Millennial Kingdom along with all of the other Kingdom saints. Their experience of being martyred during the Tribulation will be unique to the time in which they will live and die, but they will share the same general hope of all of the Old Testament saints. That they are found in heaven after having died indicates that all of the Kingdom saints who have gone before them are there as well. That they are pictured as asking the Lord to bring forth judgment on the earth indicates that they are anticipating returning with Him to receive their inheritance in His Kingdom (see Jude 14-15; Rev. 19:14-16). These martyred Kingdom saints, and all the others, who will accompany the Lord when He returns to earth are obviously waiting in heaven until the appointed time. That they are specifically said to be wearing robes and bowing before the altar in heaven tells us not only that they will continue to exist in a state of consciousness after death, but that they will also have a recognizable human form of some kind.

PRACTICAL APPLICATION FOR TODAY

The inter-dispensational principle that we learn from the story of the Rich Man and Lazarus is that it is only in this life that any man or woman has the opportunity to be reconciled to God. For those who die in unbelief, there is no second chance and there is no one to intervene on their behalf. To die without Christ is to be separated from God forever, first in the torments of Hades and finally in the Lake of Fire. As believers, this should move us with compassion for the lost and stimulate us to use every means available to proclaim the Gospel of Grace as far and wide as possible.

We also learn from this story that believers immediately enter into a better place when they leave this life at the time of physical death. Knowing that this is true provides hope and comfort both to believers who are facing death and to those they leave behind in this life.

The Lord Jesus' purpose in telling this story was to warn the self-righteous money-loving Pharisees about the consequences of trusting in the traditions of man and worldly riches rather then in the Word of God (cf. Mk. 7:5-13; Lk. 12:16-21). He also made it clear that people cannot be convinced of the truth through miracles such as someone being raised from the dead, but are to be convicted of the truth through the agency of God's Word (see Rom. 10:17; I Cor. 1:18). Those who foolishly reject the message of salvation through the Cross will die without hope, while those who accept the Gospel

The Intermediate State

as true and place their faith in Christ are reconciled to God and receive the gift of eternal life. *"For after that in the wisdom of God the world by wisdom knew not God, it pleased God by the foolishness of preaching to save them that believe"* (I Cor. 1:21). There is no one greater than *"our Savior Jesus Christ"* (Titus 2:13-14); there is no greater message than that of *"Jesus Christ and Him crucified"* (I Cor. 2:1-5); there is no greater calling than to *"the preaching of Jesus Christ, according to the revelation of the mystery"* (Rom. 16:25-27).

2

Hell, Sheol, Hades, Paradise and the Grave

There seems to be some confusion about the meaning of Hell and who goes there because of the way the Hebrew word Sheol and the Greek word Hades have been translated in our English Bibles. Since this confusion has led some into an erroneous understanding of what the Bible actually teaches about the intermediate state and the final state of the dead, we think that it is important that we address this subject here.

Sheol is found in the Bible sixty-five times. It is translated "the pit" three times, "the grave" thirty-one times, and "hell" thirty-one times. Hades is used eleven times; being rendered "hell" ten times and "grave" once. Adding to the confusion is that two other words are also translated hell in the New Testament. These are "Tartarus," which is found once and "Gehenna," which is used twelve times.

The term "Hell" is commonly understood to mean a place of torment where the souls of the wicked go after physical death. This is true. However, because Hades in the New Testament and Sheol in the Old are variously rendered hell or grave, there has been some misunderstanding about what hell and the grave are. Before looking at these words though, we should first give our attention to the Greek word Gehenna, which is always translated hell and used in reference to the Lake of Fire. It is found in Matthew 5:22,29,30; 10:28; 18:9; 23:15, 33; Mark 9:43,45,47; Luke 12:5; and James 3:6.

THE FINAL HELL

The Lake of Fire, or Hell, is a literal place of everlasting fire that was originally created by God as a place of punishment for Satan and the angels that followed him in his rebellion against God (Mat. 25:41). Because it is referred to as the place of *"outer darkness"* (Mat. 8:12; 25:30), we believe that it is most probably located at the farthest reaches of the creation. Gehenna is described in Scripture as a *"furnace of fire"* (Mat. 13:42); *"everlasting punishment"* (Mat. 25.46); *"the mist* [gloom] *of darkness"* (II Pet. 2:17); the *"hurt of the second death"* (Rev. 2:11 cf. 20:6,14; 21:8); and *"a lake of fire burning with brimstone"* (Rev. 19:20; 20:10; 21:8).

While Hell was created for Satan and the other fallen angels, the unsaved of humanity from all ages will be with them in this place of torment where *"there will be wailing and gnashing of teeth"* (Mat. 13:42). This is the "everlasting reward" of all that die in their sins.

While there is no one in the Lake of Fire at this time, it will one-day hold a vast multitude. The first residents of this place of righteous retribution will be the Beast

(Antichrist) and the False Prophet who, at the end of the Tribulation, will be *"cast alive into a lake burning with brimstone"* (Rev. 19:19-20). Joining them will be the unsaved of the nations who survive the Tribulation (Mat. 25:31-32, 41-46). Also, at Jesus Christ's return to earth, the rebel Israelites, i.e. unbelieving Jews, who survive the Tribulation, will be denied entrance into the Millennial Kingdom, no doubt to join their Gentile counterparts in the *"place of everlasting fire"* (Eze. 20:33-38; Mat. 7:21-23; cf. Mat. 24:29-31, 45-51). Then, at the end of the Millennial Kingdom of Jesus Christ, Satan will be *"cast into the lake of fire and brimstone, where the beast and the false prophet are, and shall be tormented day and night forever and ever"* (Rev. 20:10). And finally, the unsaved dead of all ages will be raised and judged at the Great White Throne by Jesus Christ and then cast into the Lake of Fire (see Rev. 20:11-15).

The name Gehenna comes from a deep narrow ravine south of Jerusalem where some Hebrew parents actually sacrificed their children to the Ammonite god, Molech, during the time of the kings (II Kin. 16:3; II Chron. 28:1-3; cf. Lev. 18:21; I Kin. 11:5,7,33). This pagan deity is also referred to as Malcham, Milcom, and Moloch in the Bible. This valley later served as the city dump and, because there was continual burning of refuse there, it became a graphic symbol of the place of punishment for the wicked. It was named the "Valley of Hinnom," which translated into Greek becomes Gehenna. The passages where the word is found in the New Testament plainly show that it was a commonly used expression for Hell by that time. The word is found twelve times in the Scriptures, being used eleven times by the Lord Jesus and once by James. When we consider the context, it is clear the Lord used this word in reference to the place of everlasting punishment for the wicked dead and not to the city dump.

Gehenna, or the Lake of Fire, might be referred to as the future, or final, Hell because it is where all of the wicked from all ages will finally end up. Satan, the fallen angels, and all of the lost of mankind will reside in torment there forever and ever.

SHEOL/HADES: THE PRESENT HELL

Scripture passages in which Gehenna is used should be distinguished from those using Hades, which refers to a place of temporary torment that we might refer to as the immediate, or present, Hell. What we mean by this is that, at the time of death, the souls of the lost go directly to Hades, where they suffer in torment until the time of the Great White Throne Judgment when they will be resurrected and cast into the Lake of Fire. The souls of all the lost who have already died are presently there and those who die in their sins immediately go there to join them.

Hades is the New Testament equivalent of the Old Testament word Sheol. The Greek and Hebrew words speak of the same place, the present Hell. However, this is problematic because Sheol has been translated "grave" as often as it has "hell" and some have mistakenly taught that Sheol and Hades are only references to the grave rather than Hell. This erroneous teaching leads to the denial of the existence of an immediate or present Hell. The false doctrine of soul-sleep, and other ideas that teach the unconscious state of the dead between death and resurrection, spring from this error.

The common word for "grave" in the Old Testament is *queber*. Of the sixty-four times it is used, it is translated "grave" thirty-four times, "sepulcher" twenty-six times, and "burying place" four times. Queber is used five additional times as part of a place name, such as Kibroth-hattaavah, which means "graves of lust." As we said earlier, Sheol is found sixty-five times, being rendered "grave" thirty-one times, "hell" thirty-one times, and "pit" three times.

A comparison of how Sheol and queber are used reveals eight points of contrast that tell us that they are not the same thing.

    1. Sheol is never used in plural form. Queber is used in the plural 29 times.

    2. It is never said that the body goes to Sheol. The body is spoken of as going to Queber 37 times.

    3. Sheol is never said to be located on the face of the earth. Queber is mentioned 32 times as being located on the earth.

4. An individual's Sheol is never mentioned. An individual's queber is mentioned 5 times.

5. Man is never said to put anyone into Sheol. Individuals are put into a queber by man 33 times.

6. Man is never said to have dug or fashioned a Sheol. Man is said to have dug, or fashioned, a queber 6 times.

7. Man is never said to have touched Sheol. Man touches, or can touch, a queber 5 times.

8. It is never said that man is able to possess a Sheol. Man is spoken of as being able to possess a queber 7 times.

(These eight points of comparison are adapted from "Life and Death" by Caleb J. Baker, Bible Institute Colportage Ass'n, 1941).

From the differences between how Sheol and queber are used in Scripture, it is obvious that they are not the same thing. The Greek word Hades in the New Testament would fit into the Sheol side of our comparison with Queber. This strongly indicating that it is the same thing as Sheol. Hades is used eleven times, being rendered Hell ten times and grave once.

Words associated with queber are "quabar" and "qeburah." Quabar is a verb meaning to bury or to be buried and qeburah is a noun meaning a grave or place of burial. The use of these related words helps to reinforce the difference between queber and Sheol, as they clearly have to do with the grave as a burial place, while Sheol does not.

EXAMPLES SHOWING THAT SHEOL IS NOT A BURIAL PLACE

After selling Joseph into slavery, his brothers stained his coat with blood and used it to convince their father that he had been killed by a wild animal (Gen. 37:26-36). Jacob's sons and daughters tried *"to comfort him; but he refused to be comforted; and he said, 'for I will go down into the grave (Sheol) unto my son mourning'. Thus his father wept for him'"* (v. 35).

From Jacob's words it is clear that he fully intended to eventually be reunited with his son in a tangible way. Obviously then, he did not simply have in mind the idea of joining him in burial as he believed that Joseph's body had not been buried at all, but was eaten by an animal (v.33). This being the case, it was impossible for Jacob to think he would join Joseph in burial. Obviously, he looked forward to being reunited with him in the place of the departed dead, not in burial. The word rendered grave in this passage is Sheol, the abode of the souls of all those who had died until Christ's resurrection.

After Jacob died, Joseph had his body mummified, a process that took forty days, then took him back to Canaan for burial (Gen. 50:1-14). When we add to that the thirty days of mourning (Gen. 50:2-4), and the time it took to travel to Canaan for the funeral (Gen. 50:5-13), we see that it was several weeks after Jacob was *"gathered unto his people"* (Gen. 49:33) before his body was placed in the cave that served as his burial place. Considering that he had been dead for well over two months before his body was buried and that the Scriptures state that at the time he died he was *"gathered to his people"* (Gen. 49:33) is telling. This shows that at the time of physical death, when *"he yielded up the spirit,"* his soul immediately departed his body to be with Isaac and Abraham. This cannot be a reference to his body being gathered together with their bodies, as that did not take place for over ten weeks. This is strong proof that Sheol does not mean a burial place for the body, but is the place where the souls of the departed reside.

That communication takes place in Sheol/Hades tells us that something other than a burial place is in view. In Isaiah 14:4-20, we find the prophet foretelling the eventual defeat and death of the king of Babylon. The nation that would eventually send Judah into captivity will itself later be defeated and its mighty king will find himself among *"the chief ones of the earth,...the kings of the nations"* (Isa. 14:9) who preceded him in death. These are the kings of nations that he had conquered with the sword and ruled over with a cruel hand (Isa. 14:6). These same men will serve as a welcoming committee for this once great "world ruler" when he arrives in Sheol/Hades. In mock surprise, they will ask this once powerful king, *"Art thou also become weak as we? Are thou become like unto us?"* (Isa. 14:10). They then taunt him by pointing out that the pretentious display of magnificence that he had demonstrated as the king of Babylon now meant nothing (Isa. 14:11).

All of those who find themselves in this section of Sheol/Hades, like the king of Babylon and the kings who greeted him, will be faced with the reality of how helpless and hopeless they are. One of the boasts these kings make against him is that, while their bodies have been placed in their respective tombs, or graves, he was not honored by a respectable burial, *"But thou are cast out of the grave* (queber) *like an abominable* (despised) *branch...thou shalt not be joined with them in burial"* (Isa. 14:18-20). Obviously, if his body was not in any grave at all, he was not simply joining them in burial.

What we see here is this man going into Sheol, while at the same time his body is cast out of its grave. Obviously then, Sheol cannot be the grave here as the body and soul are in different places, the soul going to Sheol while the body remains unburied, or outside of the grave (vs. 20) to be infested by maggots (vs. 11). It is true that this is a prophetic passage; and there are various opinions as to the identity of the person in view here (verses 12-15 are most commonly thought to refer to Satan, the power behind the Gentile kings). But, regardless of who this prophecy is about, or whether it has already been fulfilled or not, does not change the fact that Sheol and the grave are to be regarded as different places in this passage of Scripture.

THE STATE AND PLACE OF THE DEAD

In the case of Samuel and Saul, we find another example of the Scriptures making a distinction between Sheol/Hades and the grave. In his conversation with King Saul, Samuel, whom the Lord had sent back from the dead to deliver a message to Saul, said that Saul and his sons would be with him the next day (see I Sam. 28:15-19). As foretold, Saul and his sons did die the next day while in battle with the Philistines (see I Sam. 31:1-6). However, their bodies were not buried the next day so they did not join Samuel in the grave, but their souls went down to Sheol/Hades where the person, or soul, of Samuel was. As it is said that Samuel *"came up,"* it seems obvious that he went back down after speaking with Saul (I Sam. 28:8,11,14). As for the bodies of Saul and his sons, their remains were not buried for several days. As Samuel had said, they died the next day (I Sam. 31:1-6). But it was the day after they died that their bodies were taken by the Philistines and hung on the wall of Beth-Shan (I Sam. 31:7-10). After hearing of this, valiant men from Jabesh-Gilead went by night and removed their bodies, took them to Jabesh, burned them, and then buried their bones. All this took place at least three days after Saul had died, and probably longer. Saul and his sons joined Samuel in Sheol/Hades the day they died and the flesh of their bodies was burned with only their bones being placed in a grave several days later. Obviously Sheol/Hades and the grave are not the same thing, nor are they in the same place.

The story of the Rich Man and Lazarus that is found in Luke 16:19-31, as we have already seen, gives us the record of a remarkable conversation that took place in Hades between the Rich Man and Abraham. Obviously, these two men could not have had this conversation at all if Sheol/Hades is only a place where dead bodies are buried. First, there could be no communication between lifeless, decaying corpses and second, Abraham's body, which was buried in the cave of Machpelah over 1800 years earlier, had long since decayed. Also, the rich man's body, regardless of whether it had decayed or not, would not have been buried in the burial cave of Abraham. From the context, it is obvious that these men were in the place of departed souls rather than a burial place.

There are some that contend that this is a parable that never actually took place and deny that it could have ever taken place. To these, who usually hold to a position of soul-sleep or the eradication, or extinction of the soul at death, we answer; the Lord said that it did take place. Besides, as we have already pointed out, a parable by definition is a true-to-life story. To have meaning, it must be a story that could have actually taken place whether it ever did or not.

HADES IS NOT A PLACE OF SILENCE

In the effort to support the soul sleep or soul eradication theories, it has been said that Sheol/Hades is always represented in the Bible as a place of silence where there is no knowledge or communication. This simply is not so. The story of the Rich Man and Lazarus in Luke 16:19-31 clearly portrays communication taking place in Sheol/Hades and that alone makes the statement "Hades is always represented as a place of silence" obviously untrue. This is so, regardless of how one interprets this passage.

Annihilationists (who do not believe in everlasting punishment for the unsaved) also attempt to substantiate their unsound doctrine and uphold the idea that Sheol/Hades is a place of silence by using verses such as Ecclesiastes 9:10 which reads, *"there is no work, nor device, nor knowledge, nor wisdom, in the grave* (lit. Sheol).*"* However, they fail to take the context into account when they cite passages like this. Whether they do it out of ignorance or carelessness we do not know, but we do know that a verse taken out of context can often be used as a pretense. The theme of Ecclesiastes is what is done *"under the sun"* (Eccl. 1:3,9; 2:11,17; etc.), or what man can accomplish in life by his own power apart from God. When those who have lived life to the fullest, according to man's view, die, they leave nothing of true value behind and take nothing of value with them to Sheol/Hades. All that they thought was of value in this life has proven to be worthless in the end. The Book of Ecclesiastes is not concerned with what takes place after death but with what man does with his life on earth. When verses such as Ecclesiastes 9:10

are randomly lifted out of their context to build doctrine about the afterlife, serious error is sure to follow.

In the book of Jonah the prophet says that he *"prayed unto the Lord his God out of the fish's belly"* and *"out of the belly of hell* (lit. Sheol)" (Jonah 2:1-2). It seems that Jonah prayed to the Lord from the belly of the fish right after he was swallowed and was still physically alive. Then, after having died, he went to Sheol/Hades and prayed again from there before the Lord sent him back to his body, which the great fish then vomited out upon dry land (Jonah 2:10). But, regardless if one believes that Jonah died while he was in the fish's belly or not, verse two identifies Sheol/Hades as the place from which Jonah cried out to God. This is not a representation of Sheol/Hades as a place of silence but as a place from which Jonah communicated with God on a personal level.

DEATH AND SHEOL

Death and Sheol/Hades are linked together at least thirty-three times in the Scriptures. In these we see a general distinction between the "outward man," which is the body and the "inward man," which is the soul (cf. II Cor. 4:16). In this sense, death, or the grave, claims the physical part of man, the body, while Sheol/Hades claims the separated, spiritual part of man, the soul. This is exactly the meaning of Psalm 16:10: *"For Thou wilt not leave my soul in Hell* (Sheol)*; neither will Thou* *suffer Thine Holy One to see corruption."* In his Pentecostal address, Peter left no room for doubt that this was a prophetic pronouncement concerning the time between the Lord Jesus Christ's death on the Cross and His resurrection. First, he quoted Psalm 16:8-11 (Acts 2:25-28) and then made direct application of verse 10 to Christ (Acts 2:31). Not only was the Lord Jesus' soul not left in Sheol/Hades, but neither was His body left to rot in the grave. That Peter used Hades in the place of Sheol in this quotation shows that they are identical in meaning.

Of course, the Lord Jesus Christ is exceptional because He had the power not only to lay down His life on our behalf but also to take it up again (Jn. 10:17-18). This is not so of any other man as the Psalmist points out when he asks, rhetorically, *"What man is he that liveth and shall not see death? Shall he deliver his soul from the hand of the grave* (Sheol)*?"* Psalm 89:48. Because of the curse of sin, all of mankind faces the reality of physical death. None can evade it by their own power, nor can any man or woman escape from Sheol/Hades on their own. We know that since the Cross the souls of those who die *"in Christ"* do not go to Sheol/Hades but to heaven. However, this is through the merit of Jesus Christ and His power, not their own. For those *"in Christ,"* death has no sting and Sheol/Hades has no victory because their body and soul will be united in a resurrection unto life (see I Cor. 15:19-20, 51-57). This is as certain as the fact of Jesus Christ's resurrection.

This is not so for those who die without Christ for they face a resurrection unto judgment, which is referred to as the *"second death"* (Rev. 20:13-14; 21:8).

Psalm 89:48 speaks of the time when the soul is separated from the body. The body is given over to death where it will decay, while the soul is assigned to Sheol/Hades to await the final judgment. It is clear that the body and soul of the lost will be reunited at the time of the Great White Throne Judgment of the unsaved dead when *"death and Hades"* will deliver up the dead that are in them. That is, their bodies will be raised from the grave, or death, and reunited with the soul, which will come out of Sheol/Hades to be judged by Jesus Christ at the Great White Throne (see Rev. 20:11-15; cf. Jn. 5:28-29).

When the Lord Jesus said that *"as Jonah was three days and three nights in the whale's belly; so shall the Son of Man be three days and three nights in the heart of the earth"* (Mat. 12:40), He was saying that He would spend the time between His death and resurrection in Sheol/Hades. We know from Psalm 16:10 and Acts 2:25-32 that the Lord's soul, which was made an offering for sin (Isa. 53:10), was in Sheol/Hades, and we know from Matthew 12:40 that He was in the heart of the earth, which is where we believe that Sheol/Hades is located.

When we speak of the heart of something, we are not referring to that which is superficial or only skin-deep.

Symbolically, the heart signifies the innermost character, feelings, or inclinations of a man. The heart is also used when referring to the center, or core, of something. For example it is sometimes said, "the heart of a watermelon is the best part," meaning that the center part of the watermelon tastes better than the part closer to the rind. If we say that we have a "heart-felt desire" for a particular area of ministry, we would be speaking of a yearning to do the Lord's work that comes from our innermost being as opposed to a superficial desire based on the emotions of the moment. When used figuratively in the Scriptures, the word "heart" is used in a similar fashion, thus the heart of the earth gives reference to something much deeper than a simple place of burial for a man's body barely under the surface of the earth. That it is said that before His ascension the Lord Jesus first descended *"into the lower parts of the earth"* (Eph. 4:9) affirms this. In a Psalm of thanksgiving for being delivered from death, David makes reference to this by distinguishing between Sheol/Hades (rendered grave in the KJV) and Queber (rendered pit in this passage) (see Ps. 30:1-3).

In Ezekiel we find prophecies against the kings of Assyria (Ezek. 31) and Egypt (Ezek. 32) that indicate that Sheol/Hades is in the center of the earth. In these two chapters it speaks of the fall of these mighty kings, who in death ended up in the underworld with those who had gone before them. We do not have the space here to give extensive commentary on these two chapters. But, we do want to point out that in regard to both kings it is said that in death they would go *"to the nether parts of the earth...with them that go down into the pit"* (see Ezek. 31:14,16,18; 32:18, 24), the "nether parts" being the lower regions of the earth. We should take note that in chapter thirty-one it is being pointed out to Pharaoh that just as the king of Assyria, who was greater than he was, had died and gone into the underworld, so would he.

In chapter thirty-two we find a prophecy, given in the form of a lamentation, foretelling Pharaoh's defeat by the king of Babylon (Ezek. 32:1-16). This is followed by a lamentation over the multitude of Egyptians who would be slain by the Babylonians (Ezek. 31:17-31). We have pictured for us those of the nations who preceded them welcoming Pharaoh and his host as they arrived in Sheol/Hades by taunting them. They point out that the Egyptians had thought themselves to be invincible because of their strength and fame among the nations. But now they were just like the great nations who had gone before them, their individual souls being confined to Sheol/Hades while their bodies' decay in the grave.

"The strong among the mighty shall speak to him out of the midst of hell (Sheol)...." (Ezek. 32:21). The *"strong among the mighty"* spoken of here refers to the men who had been the kings and leaders of the different nations that are mentioned in this passage; Asshor, or Assyria

(Vv. 22), Elam (Vv. 24), Meshech and Tubal (Vv. 26), Edom, her kings and her princes (Vv. 29), the princes of the north and the Zidonians (Vv. 30). This passage shows that while those of each group mentioned are in their respective burial places, their quebers, they are at the same time all together in *"the pit,"* which is an expression that is sometimes used for Sheol/Hades (Vv. 18,25,29). These examples are similar to what is found in Isaiah 14, which we have previously looked at.

While we have not exhausted the subject by looking at every passage that Sheol is found in, it is clear from these examples that Sheol is not simply the grave but is located at the center of the earth and is the abode of the souls of the unrighteous dead who are awaiting their resurrection unto condemnation. It is equally clear that those in Sheol/Hades are not in an unconscious state of existence but are quite aware of what is going on around them. There is memory, recognition, and communication there.

TARTARUS

The Apostle Peter used the word Tartarus in reference to *"the angels that sinned"* that God delivered to Sheol/Hades to await judgment (II Pet. 2:4). This word, which is translated *"hell"* in the KJV, was used in Greek mythology to refer to the place of punishment for the most wicked. It is not clear if Peter was using this word in reference to Sheol/Hades in a general way or if he was referring to a specific compartment of Sheol/Hades where a certain class of fallen angels are confined awaiting final judgment. Either way, this passage teaches that there is a place of confinement in which a particular group of beings are being held until the time of their judgment. This is consistent with the overall Biblical teaching about the existence and purpose of Sheol/Hades.

PARADISE

While Paradise is not now a part of Sheol/Hades it will be mentioned here because it was located in Sheol/Hades at one time. Before the death, burial, and resurrection of Jesus Christ everybody who died went to Sheol/Hades, which was at that time divided into at least two compartments. One was a place of torment while the other was a place of blessing, which was referred to as Abraham's Bosom (Lk. 16:22-25). As we mentioned before, Tartarus may be a specific place in Sheol/Hades.

We know that Jesus Christ went *"into the lower parts of the earth"* (Eph. 4:9), that is to Sheol/Hades *"in the heart of the earth,"* for three days and nights while his body was in the grave (Mat. 12:40). The Lord Jesus told the repentant thief that he would join Him in Paradise that same day (Lk. 23:42-43). This tells us that Paradise was located in Sheol/Hades at that time. We believe that this was the same place referred to as Abraham's Bosom in Luke 16. However, after Jesus Christ rose from the dead, He ascended to the Father, taking the saints who were in Abraham's Bosom to heaven with Him. Thus, He took *"captivity captive"* (see Eph. 4:8-10).

That Paradise was moved to heaven is confirmed to us by the Apostle Paul who speaks of a man who was *"caught up into Paradise"* where he *"heard unspeakable words"* (II Cor. 12:3-4). With Jesus Christ's work complete, the believers who had been confined to Sheol/Hades were now taken to Heaven to wait in God's presence until the time of their resurrection to enter His Kingdom on Earth. Since that time, at death, all believers go to Paradise in Heaven to await the time of their resurrection. This is true whether they belong to the Kingdom Church of the future or the Body of Christ Church of the present Dispensation of Grace whose members will be resurrected at the Rapture.

THE GRAVE

We have already looked at the word queber, the most common word for grave, or a burial place, in the Old Testament, and have shown that it is not the same as Sheol. As previously stated, of the sixty-four times it is used it is rendered "grave" thirty-four times, "sepulcher" twenty-six times, and "burying place" four times. Two other words that are used for a burial place in the Old Testament are *shah-ghath* and *qeburah*.

Shah-ghath: This word is translated "grave" once (Job 33:22). It is rendered "ditch" twice, "destruction" twice, "corruption" four times, and "pit" thirteen times. This word speaks of something that man can dig (Ps. 94:13; Prov. 26:27) and is used in reference to a hole into which a man can fall (Ps. 7:15; Prov. 26:27), and a hole used as a trap (Ps. 35:7). It is a place where the physical body suffers destruction through the corruption of decay (Ps. 16:10; 49:9; 55:23). The basic meaning is that of a hole of some kind that man digs for a particular purpose. Generally, it is used of a burial place, i.e., a grave.

Qeburah: This word is related to queber and means a grave or burial place. It is used of various types of graves and is found fourteen times and is translated "grave" four times, "sepulcher" five times, "burial" four times, and "burying place" one time.

In the New Testament we find three more words that refer to the grave, *taphos, mnema,* and *mnemeion*.

Taphos is used seven times and is translated "sepulcher" six of those and "tomb" once.

Mnema is used seven times, being rendered "tomb" twice, "grave" once, and "sepulcher" four times.

Mnemeion is the most common word for grave in the New Testament. It is used forty-two times, five times as "tomb," twenty-nine times as "sepulcher," and eight times as "grave."

The grave is a place where the physical remains of those who have died are deposited. It can be a hole in the ground, a cave, or a specially prepared vault or other place used for interment. The soul and spirit having departed the body at death, there is no consciousness of life in the grave. It is a place of corruption that serves to point out man's need of a Savior. The soul of man lives on after physical death and will always remain in a conscious state of being. The unsaved go to Sheol/Hades to await their resurrection unto condemnation, while the redeemed go to heaven to await their resurrection unto life (see Jn. 5:25-29; Dan. 12:2).

OTHER ARGUMENTS

Here we want to deal briefly with some other arguments that have been raised against the position taken in this booklet, which is the continued conscious existence of the individual after physical death. Some of these arguments have come as feedback from our previous writings on this subject, and some we have discovered during our research. What we believe is a consistent pattern among those who believe in the unconscious state of the soul after physical death (whether soul sleep or the eradication of the soul), is that, when their position is threatened by a passage of Scripture, they simply change its meaning to agree with their belief and claim to have resolved the issue. Obviously, those who deny the immortality of the human soul cannot accept at face value the plain statements of Scripture that teach otherwise so, when confronted with the testimony of God's Word, they must either change the Scriptures or change their minds. Sadly, some would rather revise the Bible than admit the truth.

The Lower Parts of the Earth: In Ephesians 4:7-10, Jesus Christ is said to have *"descended first into the lower parts of the earth"* taking *"captivity captive"* and then ascended into heaven. We believe that *"the lower parts of the earth"* is a reference to Sheol/Hades, which is in the center of the earth. Those who deny the continued conscious existence of the soul after death cannot allow this to mean Sheol/Hades because their position denies that it even exists, claiming that Sheol and Hades are only references to the grave. They say that this passage only refers to Jesus Christ's incarnation, that is His coming to dwell on the face of the earth where man lives out his day-to-day life, and that it has no connection with any subterranean realm of any kind. Psalm 139:13-15 is given as a proof text for this position.

The term *"the lowest parts of the earth"* is found in Psalm 139:15, but this passage does not prove that Sheol/Hades is not in the center of the earth or that Jesus Christ did not go there. Here this term is not referring to the earth but is a poetic reference to the womb of the writer's mother where he was out of the sight of man but was not hid from God. Yes, the conception and development of the writer (David) in his mother's womb did take place on the face of the earth, but the analogy is that of a place hidden from man but known to God. It is not in reference to the surface of the earth, and it most certainly does not picture the grave as it speaks of the development of life and vitality, not death and decay.

However, the idea of a subterranean place such as the traditional Sheol/Hades could be in view as an analogy. This passage actually does nothing to refute a literal interpretation of Luke 16:19-31 or the traditional view that Ephesians 4:8-9 refers to Christ's death, decent into Sheol/Hades, His resurrection and exaltation. Regardless, there are other passages of Scripture that use the phrase *"the lower parts of the earth"* that should also be considered.

Psalm 63:9-10 reads, *"But those that seek my soul, to destroy it, shall go into the lower parts of the earth. They shall fall by the sword: they shall be a portion for foxes."* Since both the Psalmist and those seeking his life were already living on the face of the earth, *"the lower parts of the earth"* in this passage obviously refers to some other place that they could go to. It can't simply mean the grave though because, when they were killed by the sword, the bodies of those who were to be consigned to the *"lower parts of the earth"* were to be left for scavengers to devour (*"they shall be a portion for foxes"*). There can be little doubt that this is a reference to Sheol/Hades, which is in the center, or lowest, part of the earth.

In Isaiah 44:23, *"the lower parts of the earth"* is definitely used as a reference to the face of the earth. However, it is not used in regard to the earth in general but of specific terrain found on the earth. Here it refers to the lower portions of the landscape in contrast to the highest. In other words, the mountains and the valleys.

This portion of Scripture poetically pictures the heavens and all parts of the earth singing and shouting of the goodness and glory of God for redeeming Israel. The use of the phrase *"the lower parts of the earth"* here neither confirms or denies either view of Ephesians 4:8-9.

Ezekiel 31 and 32 both contain references to *"the nether parts of the earth"* (Ezek. 31:14,16,18; 32:18,24). Although it is translated different in Ezekiel than it is in Psalms and Isaiah ("nether" instead of "lower" is used), the same Hebrew words are found in all three books.

We have already taken a brief look at these chapters under the heading "Death and Sheol," but we will revisit them here. These prophecies against the kings of Assyria (Ezek. 31) and Egypt (Ezek. 32) indicate that Sheol/Hades is in the center of the earth. It speaks of the fall of these mighty kings who, in death, ended up in the underworld with those who had gone before them. We do not have the space here to give an extensive commentary on these two chapters. But, we do want to point out that, in regard to both kings, it is said that in death they would go *"to the nether parts of the earth...with them that go down into the pit."* (see Ezek. 31:14,16,18; 32:18,24), the *"nether parts"* being the lower regions, or the depths, of the earth. We should take note that in chapter thirty-one it is being pointed out to Pharaoh that just as the king of Assyria, who was greater than he, had died and gone into the underworld, so would he.

In chapter thirty-two, a prophecy is given in the form of a lamentation, foretelling Pharaoh's defeat by the king of Babylon (Ezek. 32:1-6). This is followed by a lamentation over the multitudes of Egyptians who would be slain by the Babylonians (Ezek. 31:17-31). We have pictured for us those of the nations who preceded them welcoming Pharaoh and his host as they arrived in Sheol/Hades by taunting them. In their taunts, they point out that the Egyptians had previously thought themselves to be something special because of their great strength and fame among the nations. But, now they were just like those who had gone before them. Their individual souls were confined to Sheol/Hades, along with those they had conquered, while their bodies decayed in the grave. These passages of Scripture clearly show that Sheol/Hades and the grave are not the same thing. They give strong support to the view that Ephesians 4:8-9 refers to Jesus Christ's descent into Sheol/Hades while His Body was in the grave between His death on the Cross and His resurrection.

The Captivity Led Captive: Paul's quote of Psalm 68:18 in Ephesians 4:8 is said to be a reference to Moses freeing the captive Israelites from bondage in Egypt, which Paul used as an illustration of Jesus Christ freeing the members of the Body of Christ from bondage to sin. Those holding this view insist that the passage has nothing to do with the Lord descending into Sheol/Hades and removing the souls of the departed saints

Hell, Sheol, Hades, Paradise and the Grave

from that place and transferring them to heaven when He ascended to the Father after His resurrection. However, the subject of this passage is not Moses going up to the heights of Mt. Sinai. Yes, the shaking of Mt. Sinai when the Law was given to Moses is mentioned (Ps. 68:7-8) but, in verse sixteen, the subject has become *"the hill which God desireth to dwell in; yea the Lord will dwell in it forever"* (Ps. 68:16). This can only mean Jerusalem (Deut. 12:5-7; II Chron. 6:5-6). It is similar in that the Lord's presence is said to be manifested in the Holy Place as it was at Sinai (Ps. 68:17), but it was clearly written with the Temple at Jerusalem in view (Ps. 68:28-29). Psalm 68 is a prophetic anticipation of the Lord's victory and triumph over Israel's enemies. At that still future time, those of Israel who are dispersed among the nations in the captivity of "exile from the Promised Land," will be gathered together and brought into the land of their fathers. Thus, the Psalmist speaks of the Lord Jesus Christ taking this *"captivity captive"* that He might take them to their homeland. The natural illustration that we get from this Psalm is one of deliverance from a place of isolation from the Lord's personal presence to being brought into His holy habitation. This is in complete harmony with the overall teaching of the Scriptures on this subject. At the end of the Tribulation, the Lord will re-gather all of the Israelite people and bring them to the land of Israel. Jerusalem, where the Temple was, and will be again located, *"is the hill which God desireth to dwell in"* (Ps. 68:16). In

Jeremiah, the Lord refers to the dispersed of Israel as the captivity (Jer. 30:3; 33:6-8). This goes beyond the 70 year Babylonian captivity, from which only a remnant of the Israelites ever returned, to Christ's Second Coming and all of Israel's return to the Promised Land. It is important to note that all the tribes of Israel are mentioned in these and other prophetic passages that deal with the subject. Our whole basis for a dispensational understanding of the Bible is built around the fact that all Israel will one day be re-gathered in the Promised Land where they will enjoy the blessing of the presence of God in the Person of the Lord Jesus Christ.

The point the Apostle Paul is making by using the illustration of God's people, who were exiled from His presence in the Temple at Jerusalem, being apprehended by the Lord and taken back to the Promised Land to enjoy His presence forever is to show that after His death, burial, and resurrection the Lord took the departed believers of the past as His personal captives and ushered them out of their captivity in Sheol/Hades and into heaven to enjoy the blessing of being in the presence of God. Even if Psalm 68 is only about Israel's return to Jerusalem to rebuild the Temple after 70 years in Babylon, the principle of the illustration is the same.

The Opinions of Most Bible Commentators: In an effort to defend their view of Luke 16:19-31, some who believe in soul sleep, or in soul eradication, point out that many Bible commentaries say it is a parable. While it is true that many commentaries do say that the story of the Rich Man and Lazarus is a parable rather than a literal historical account, this fact does not prove that it is a parable or that it is not a parable. It only proves that there is a difference of opinion between Bible commentators on this point which, of course, we already know. What is more important to the issue at hand is how those who see it as a parable interpret its meaning.

In the many commentaries, theologies, and other works that we have consulted, a substantial majority believe that Luke 16:19-31 teaches the continued conscious state of the soul between death and resurrection. This is true of both those who believe it is a historical account and those who believe it is a parable.

For the most part, the difference between those who see it as a parable and those who do not is their approach to Bible interpretation. Generally, those who are Covenant and/or Reformed in their theology are more apt to see it as a parable because they are more allegorical in their methods of the interpretation of Scripture. On the other hand, those who are Dispensational in their understanding of Scripture see it as a historical account because they are more literal in their approach to interpreting the Bible and accept the account at face value. Our point here is that regardless of their theological bias, the vast majority of Bible believing commentators, scholars, theologians, and teachers believe that the story of the Rich Man and Lazarus teaches the continued conscious existence of the soul of man between death and the resurrection of the body. Those who hold to the historical view do so because they believe it is plainly taught in this passage as well as other parts of the Bible. Those who believe that it is a parable do so because they recognize that the story illustrates a truth that is taught in other parts of the Bible.

Regardless of the percentages concerning the number of commentaries that see Luke 16:19-31 as a parable as opposed to the number that view it as a historical account, the evidence from the consensus of opinion of most Bible teachers is that the human soul is immortal and it continues to exist as a individual entity in a state of consciousness between physical death and resurrection. They may claim it, but the soul sleep/soul eradication proponents can produce no actual evidence from this line of reasoning to support their view. In reality, their position is refuted even by most of those who agree that Luke 16:19-31 should be considered a parable.

Being regenerated by the Holy Spirit when saved through faith in Christ for the forgiveness of sins (Titus 3:5; Rom. 3:24-25), every believer is made spiritually alive (Eph. 2:1,5) and sealed until the day of redemption (Eph. 1:13-14), given everlasting life (I Tim. 1:16), and the love of God is poured into their hearts by the Holy Spirit, which is given unto them (Rom. 5:5). God, who cannot lie (Titus 1:2), has promised in His Word that nothing, not even death, can separate any blood-bought saint from His love, *"which is in Christ Jesus our Lord"* (see Rom. 8:35-39). Not a thing in all of creation can bring to nothing the life given as a gift from God because it is eternal. With the utmost confidence in God's infallible Word, every believer can say with the Apostle Paul *"to live is Christ and to die is gain."*

PRACTICAL APPLICATION FOR TODAY

A proper understanding of what the Bible teaches about Hell, Sheol, Hades, and the Grave dispels confusion over what happens to the soul at the time of physical death and guards against being led astray by those teaching the false doctrines of soul-sleep, eradication of the soul, the universal reconciliation of mankind, and the annihilation of the lost. All of these erroneous doctrines are used of Satan to dishearten believers and blind the lost to the reality of the cost of spurning the Gospel of Jesus Christ. Our thinking, and therefore our life on a day to day basis, is influenced by what we believe. While some of the false doctrines mentioned above are diametrically opposed to each other, they still have one thing in common; they subvert the truth of the immortality of the soul and dilute the Gospel of Jesus Christ.

3

The Resurrections and Judgments

There are three different resurrections and seven judgments spoken of in the Bible. It is important to distinguish between them because failure to do so invariably leads to a misunderstanding of what will take place in the future. There are many who assume that there is one final judgment day on which everybody will be judged to see if they have been good enough to get into heaven or not. Nothing could be farther from the truth, but multitudes are trying to earn their way into heaven because they do not know the truth.

THE RESURRECTIONS

The Mystery Resurrection: This resurrection is only mentioned in the epistles of the Apostle Paul. It will occur at the time of the Rapture of the Body of Christ, which will mark the end of the Dispensation of Grace and the re-emergence of the prophetic Kingdom program. Only those who became believers during the Dispensation of Grace will take part in the resurrection. This resurrection is the first to take place, but, it is not the First Resurrection. Some principle passages of Scripture that pertain to this resurrection are I Corinthians 15:51-58; Philippians 3:20-21; and I Thessalonians 4:13-18. Those in this resurrection will occupy heaven.

The First Resurrection: This resurrection is the first in the prophetic time. Unlike the Mystery Resurrection, which was a secret until the Lord revealed it to the Apostle Paul, the First Resurrection is the subject of prophecy. It will take place at the end of the Tribulation (Rev. 20:4-6). Those who are in this resurrection will enter the Millennial Kingdom of Jesus Christ on earth. This is the *"Resurrection of Life"* spoken of by the Lord Jesus in John 5:27.

The Second Resurrection: This is the final resurrection. It will take place at the end of the Millennial Kingdom. All of the unsaved dead of all ages will be in this resurrection. They will be judged at the Great White Throne Judgment and cast into the Lake of Fire (Rev. 20:11-15). This final resurrection is the *"Resurrection of Damnation"* spoken of by the Lord Jesus in John 5:29.

THE JUDGMENTS

The Judgment of the Sins of the World on the Cross: This took place when Jesus Christ took the sins of the world upon Himself and suffered God's judgment for those sins when He died as our substitute (II Cor. 5:21; Gal. 3:13). This judgment makes it possible for the Father to forgive sins and impute righteousness to those

The Resurrections and Judgments

who trust in the Son for redemption (Eph. 1:6-7). This judgment is universal only in the sense that Christ was sufficient to save any and everyone who puts their trust in Him for salvation. Only those who believe receive forgiveness of their sins.

The Believer's Self-Judgment: Judgment has to do with conviction and repentance. Conviction takes place when believers, through the testimony of God's Word and the indwelling Holy Spirit, realize that there are one or more areas of their life not in accord with God's will for them. Judgment takes place when the believer who is under conviction acknowledges in his or her own mind and heart that whatever thought, attitude, or action that they are convicted of is wrong, and it leads them to repentance. Repentance takes place when they turn from whatever it is they are convicted of to seek God's will in this area of life. An example of this is the immoral man of I Corinthians 5:1-5 who was put out of the church until he came to his senses and, in godly sorrow over his misdeeds, repented and was restored to fellowship (II Cor. 2:6-8). Actually the entire Corinthian church in general was involved in self-judgment as they responded as individuals to Paul's admonishment about their divisive spirit and careless attitude about sin within the church (see I Cor. 1:10-31; 5:1-6:20 with II Cor. 2:1-8; 7:2-16).

The Judgment of the Believer's Works: This judgment will take place at the *"Judgment Seat of Christ"*

(II Cor. 5:10). The believer's works, not his sins, will be judged at this judgment. Every believer's works as a member of the Body of Christ will be evaluated as to what sort they were. Only that which is done in faith will be considered for rewards. The works of the flesh will be burned up as *"wood, hay, and stubble,"* while what is done in faith will result in rewards that the Apostle Paul pictures as *"gold, silver, and precious stones"* because of their enduring and great value (I Cor. 3:10-15; cf. Rom. 14:10,12; II Cor. 5:10; Gal. 6:4-5; etc.).

Undoubtedly there will be a sense of remorse by some believers at the time of this judgment because of their unfaithfulness to the Lord. Nevertheless, every believer will acknowledge God's goodness towards them and will *"glory in the Lord"* (I Cor. 1:30-31).

The Judgment of Israel: At the time of Jesus Christ's return to earth, all of the Jews who have survived the Tribulation will be gathered together out of all the nations into the wilderness and the true believers will be separated from the unbelieving Jews (Eze. 20:33-38; Mat. 7:21-23). This is the separation of the wheat from the chaff spoken of by John the Baptist (Mat. 4:11-12) and the meaning of the parable of the wheat and the tares (Mat. 13:24-30). This judgment will take place before the Judgment of the Nations.

The Judgment of the Nations: At the beginning of the Millennial Kingdom, all of the Gentiles who have survived the Tribulation (at least three quarters of the world population will die during the preceding seven years of great trouble on earth) will be judged as *"sheep"* and *"goats"* by Christ as He sits on *"the throne of glory"* (Mat. 25:31-46). Those judged to be *"sheep"* nations will be allowed into the Millennial Kingdom (Mat. 25:34), and those judged to be *"goat"* nations will be assigned to the unending torments of *"everlasting fire"* (Mat. 25:41). This Judgment of the Gentiles will be based on how they treat Christ's *"brethren"* during the Tribulation (Mat. 25:40,45). The basis of those judgments is the Abrahamic Covenant (Gen. 12:1-3).

The Judgment of the Unsaved Dead: At the end of Jesus Christ's one thousand year reign on earth, the unsaved of all of the dead will be resurrected to stand before the Great White Throne where Christ will judge them according to their works and then cast them into the Lake of Fire (Rev. 20:11-15). This judgment is associated with the *"Resurrection of Damnation"* (Jn. 5:29 cf. Dan. 12:2) and will determine the degree of suffering of the lost in the Lake of Fire. Only unsaved individuals will face this judgment.

The Judgment of Angels: We do not find much about this judgment in Scripture. However, we do know that some fallen angels have already been bound with chains in Hades to await their final judgment (II Pet. 2:4; Jude 6). We also know that Satan will be bound with a chain and cast into the Bottomless Pit (Hades) for one thousand years before being set free and permitted to again influence the nations against God. This will only be for a short time (Rev. 20:1-3, 7-9) after which he will be cast into the Lake of Fire (Rev. 20:10). As Satan will be bound in the Bottomless Pit during the peaceful time of the Millennial Kingdom, it stands to reason that all of the other fallen angels (demons) will be there with him. It seems most probable that they will be released with him to help deceive the nations and then cast into the Lake of Fire with him when his last rebellion is put down (Rev. 20:7-10). This seems even more likely when we take into consideration the fact that at the middle of the Tribulation, Satan and all of his angels will be cast out of heaven together (Rev. 12:7-9). Regardless if the scenario just outlined is correct or not, we do know without a doubt that Satan and his angels will all finally end up in the Lake of Fire, as the place of *"everlasting fire"* was originally prepared for them (Mat. 25:41).

A GENERAL LOOK AT THE NATURE OF JUDGMENT IN THE OLD TESTAMENT

In looking at the idea of everlasting judgment in the Old Testament, we must remember that for Israel, entering into Messiah's glorious Kingdom is the equivalent of the Body of Christ going to heaven. To permanently dwell in the land in a state of perpetual peace and prosperity is the inheritance of their Messianic hope. Their going on into the blessed state of the new earth after the final judgment is a continuance of their inheritance (see

The Resurrections and Judgments

Rev. 20:11-21:8). Keeping that in mind, we have cited over twenty passages from the Old Testament in the following list that speak of judgment with a brief statement regarding what is said in them about the fate of the wicked. The point is that no hope is offered to them.

Numbers 24:20,24 – Evil doers have no hope.

Deuteronomy 7:9-10 – God gives mercy to them that love Him and brings to destruction those who hate Him.

Psalm 1:1-6 – The ungodly are opposite of the righteous.

9:5,15-17 – The name of the heathen is put out forever by his being put into Hell.

37:27-29,38-40 – The righteous and wicked contrasted with the righteous saved and the wicked cut off.

49:6-9 – There is a time when the opportunity for redemption of the soul comes to an end.

49:17-19 – Those not redeemed by God will never see "the light" (literally = the light of Life) Note: this is in contrast to those God does redeem and receive as His own (v. 15).

55:22-23 – The righteous will be sustained while the wicked are brought down into the pit of destruction (also see II Peter 1:4).

75:8-10 – A contrast of opposites between the judgment of the righteous and the wicked.

78:66 – Perpetual, or everlasting, reproach is the fate of God's enemies.

81:15 – The fate of those who hate God is everlasting.

83:17 – Everlasting shame and dismay for God's enemies.

92:4-7 – The wicked are destroyed forever.

Proverbs 10:25 – The wicked will not be on the everlasting foundation.

10:28-30 – Destruction to the workers of iniquity, and the wicked have no hope and will not inherit the land.

11:7 – The hope of the wicked and unjust ends at death.

11:29-31 – the righteous will be rewarded accordingly and also the wicked and the sinner.

14:32 – Unlike the wicked, the righteous have hope in death.

Isaiah 33:14 – Hypocrites rightly fear and worry about going into the everlasting fire.

45:16-17 – The everlasting salvation of Israel is in direct contrast to the shame, disgrace, and confusion of idolaters. Neither will ever come to an end.

51:6-8 – The righteous will be in the New Heavens and the New Earth, while others are eaten by moths and worms (cf. Mk. 9:43-48).

66:22-24 – As long as the New Heavens and New Earth remain, the transgressors will remain in the place of unquenchable fire.

Daniel 12:1-2 – How much plainer could it be that the righteous will have everlasting life, while the unrighteous will suffer everlasting abhorrence? (also see Jn. 5:28-29; Rev. 20:4-5;11-15; cf. Rev. 14:10-11; I Thess. 4:13-18; II Thess. 1:7-9).

4

Universalism and Annihilationism

Two false doctrines that believers need to be aware of are Universalism and Annihilationism as they come to the forefront of theological debate from time to time. And when they do they usually find their way into the pulpit as well.

Universalism teaches that every human being will eventually be saved from the penalty of sin to live eternally in personal communion with God. Annihilationism, on the other hand, believes that those who die in their sins will at some point completely cease to exist as their soul will be annihilated after suffering the appropriate punishment for their sins in Hell. While these two views seem to be complete opposites, they have much in common in regards to the basic premise that they are built on. Proponents of both views claim that a God of love would never condemn anyone to everlasting punishment in such a horrible place as the Lake of Fire. One has chosen to believe that eventually everyone will be saved, the other that the souls of unbelievers will eventually be eradicated, thus ending their existence. Both deny that the Lake of Fire, or Hell, is a place of everlasting punishment.

THE DOCTRINE OF UNIVERSALISM

We can understand why people would want to believe in Universal Reconciliation because it is troubling to think about individuals suffering in Hell forever. But, it is hard to understand how those who claim to believe in the authority of the Bible as the inerrant Word of God can come to the conclusion that the Scriptures teach Universalism. When the Bible is simply taken at face value, it is obvious that there is a vast difference in the final condition of those who die in faith and those who die in their sins.

Ignoring or changing clear statements that teach otherwise, Universalists search for verses that they think teach their view and go to great lengths in their word studies to try to prove it. But, they offer no definitive passage of Scripture that clearly supports what they teach. Without such a passage, they actually have no case for their doctrine.

No essential truth of Scripture is hidden away to be found only in incidental remarks or passages that, even after being thoroughly studied, remain unclear or cryptic in nature. And, as *"Christ Jesus came into the world to save sinners"* (I Tim. 1:15), we should expect the why, who and how of salvation, and the fate of the saved and unsaved to be clearly stated in Scripture. We believe that this is what we find in the Bible.

It is clearly stated in Scripture that the whole world, all human beings, are sinners who are only worthy of

Universalism & Annihilationism

the judgment of death (Rom. 1:28-32; 3:19-20,23); that Jesus Christ came to be a propitiation to satisfy our sin debt through His death (Rom. 3:24-25; I Cor. 15:3-4); and that God has promised to save all of those who believe the message of the Cross (Rom. 3:26; I Cor. 1:18-21; Eph. 1:13-14).

We also find it said that all of the unsaved, whose names are *"not found written in the Book of Life,"* will be finally *"cast into the Lake of Fire"* (Rev. 20:15), which is a place where those who inhabit it *"shall be tormented day and night forever and ever"* (Rev. 20:10). But, there is no verse that says that anyone who is cast into the Lake of Fire will ever be removed or that offers them any hope of a second chance or opportunity to escape. When Universalists teach otherwise, they are teaching heresy, dangerous heresy.

Universalism encompasses a wide range of adherents. Those holding to a relativist view generally believe that all paths eventually lead to some form or other of eternal bliss, or oneness with God, regardless of what a person believes. This is a common belief among New Age and other pantheistic and polytheistic religions as well as by some who claim to be Christian. Those holding this view most often understand God to be a divine force of some kind rather than the Personal God that the Bible reveals Him to be.

In contrast, most "professing" Christians who are proponents of Universalism usually say that since Jesus

Christ's death on the Cross was for the sins of the world, its effect must be universal, resulting in the salvation from the penalty of sin unto eternal life of every person. This idea is mostly found among the liberal denominations where the love of God is stressed and His holiness played down, but it is found among Evangelicals also.

The co-mingling of the ideas of Universalism with the teachings of the Bible can be traced back to an early church leader named Origen who lived about A.D. 185-254. A strong proponent, Hosea Ballou (1771-1852), can be credited with the advancement of Universalism in the United States. His writings indicate that he was influenced by Rationalism. He taught that God created sin, that humanity is basically good, that the Lord Jesus' death was not substitutionary, and denied Christ's full deity. In recent years, there has been a surge of Universalist teachings among Evangelicals in America.

In looking at the beliefs of Universalism, it should be asked; what is the Gospel Message and how should it be presented to the lost? How would a true Universalist answer the question that the Philippian jailer asked the Apostle Paul: *"what must I do to be saved?"* (Acts 16:30). Paul simply said *"believe on the Lord Jesus Christ, and thou shalt be saved"* (Acts 16:31). But, to hold true to the doctrine of Universalism, this answer is incomplete.

If asked this important question, to give a comprehensive answer the Universalist would have to say something like this; "You can believe on Jesus Christ now and be saved by His sin cleansing blood or you can continue in your unbelief and after you die you will be purified from your sins in the fires of Hell before entering into eternal life. You have no choice; you will be saved whatever you do. The only choice you have is to be saved through Christ's blood in this life or to die in your sins and suffer for them yourself in the Lake of Fire before you can go to heaven."

Now, I am sure that the Universalists would argue that I am misrepresenting their position and insist that they believe that the blood of Jesus Christ will save all of mankind. But, their belief in a temporal Hell where those who die in their sins go to undergo remedial suffering that prepares them for eternal life denies that. Either Christ's suffering for the sins of mankind on the Cross was necessary for anyone to be saved or it wasn't really necessary at all. If people who die in their sins can suffer any punishment in Hell at all for those sins to make them ready for heaven, then the shedding of Christ's blood was not necessary at all. The whole point of the Gospel is that through faith alone in Christ's blood alone sinful men and women can be saved, or delivered, from the judgment of a righteous God. The idea of Hell only being a correctional facility where nothing but a remedial punishment is administered is an affront to Jesus Christ and what He did on the Cross. If anyone can in any way make themselves righteous before God through good works or by paying for their own sins through suffering, the Cross is a mockery of justice and an insult to all of those who have sacrificed their lives for the sake of the Gospel.

According to Universalism, the sufficiency of the blood of Jesus Christ is not exclusively applied to those who believe on Christ for salvation, but will be universally applied to all of mankind resulting in a universal salvation of all men and women. They say this in spite of the fact that the Bible says that only those who believe will be saved (see Rom. 3:23-26). To get around that truth, Universalism says that, after suffering in Hell, those who died in their sins will finally believe and be saved. They use isolated Scripture verses to support this but, as we have said before, they offer no passage of Scripture that can be expounded in its context that supports this idea. This leaves their doctrine with nothing to support it but conjecture.

Universalists often bring up the question, "why would God create man in the first place if He knew that most of mankind would end up in Hell forever?" They seem to think that this question, which is based on philosophy rather than Scripture, cannot be adequately answered and therefore proves their point. We disagree but, before addressing that question, we would ask the Universalists a question of our own. Since God knew about all of the evil and suffering that would take place in a fallen world, why did He allow sin to come into His

Universalism & Annihilationism

good creation in the first place? If God is going to save all of the human race anyway, what is the purpose of Him tolerating thousands of years of evil being perpetrated by the human race; wickedness that has resulted in gross physical suffering and mental anguish for vast multitudes? Rampant crime and mayhem, the destruction of war, the helpless continually being exploited, the powerful forcing their evil will on the masses, and the list could go on and on, has been the usual throughout the centuries.

Since, as Universalists claim, God's plan is to save all of mankind anyway, why didn't He just create man in perfect righteousness to start with and never allow sin to enter in and corrupt the whole creation? After all, since He loves man and hates sin, what difference would it make in the long run? Wouldn't that really have been a better plan then to allow the blight of sin and the suffering it has caused to affect the human race the way it has since shortly after the time of Creation? Human wisdom would say so, but obviously God in His infinite wisdom didn't think so, did He?

But, going back to the original question, I would like to offer the opinion that the answer is that if man was to have a personal relationship with God, it had to be based on the freedom to choose. Yes, God can and does alter circumstances and situations and intervene in the affairs of men, but He does not force any individual into a loving personal relationship with Himself. There has to be a personal freewill response to the love offered to enter into that kind of relationship. He has done what He has done for our sake, that we might have the opportunity to accept, or reject, His love. Universalism minimizes the relational aspect of what it means to be "in Christ." One enters into this relationship with God through faith, and faith comes from hearing the Word of God, not through the fires of Hell as Universalism would have us believe. Doctrine must not be determined through this kind of philosophical speculation, but only by trusting in what the Bible actually says.

If the Universalist version of the Gospel were presented to the non-Christian, why would they trust in Christ? What incentive would there be for a Hindu or Muslim living in an area that is openly hostile towards Christianity, and even has laws against converting from their religion to Christianity, become a Christian? Let's say it is a man with a wife and three children and he knows that if he professes to be a Christian he will be persecuted and possibly even killed. In addition, his wife and children will almost certainly suffer as well. His sons will be expelled from school and have a hard time finding employment and his young daughter might be kidnapped and sold into slavery or forced into prostitution. Or the whole family could be killed.

Such a man may have seen Christian love demonstrated by those witnessing to him and feel remorse for his sinful ways and even be touched by the Gospel.

But, he believes that there is no real danger of losing his soul because he has been convinced that the Bible teaches that he and all of his family will end up in heaven with Jesus Christ eventually anyway. So, as he sees it, his choice is to either become a Christian now and bring suffering on himself and his whole family or reject Christ so he and his family can continue in their traditional religion and their sinful lifestyle and then suffer for a season after they die and still be saved. All he would be trading would be a better life now for the possibility of a reward for faithfulness for having believed and served God in this life. Besides, he would probably conclude that if his religion is right, he will be better off not becoming a Christian and if not he will still be saved. Almost certainly he will choose to simply remain as he is. There are no examples from Scripture or from history to suggest otherwise. On the other hand, great in number are the testimonies of those who, through *"the preaching of the Cross,"* have become convicted of their sin and turned to Jesus Christ as their Savior from the horrors of an everlasting Hell that they knew they deserved. And many of these came to faith in Christ while facing almost certain persecution and/or death. The historical record also shows that the preachers, evangelists, and missionaries that God has used in the past are those who boldly preached *"Christ crucified,"* offering eternal life to those who believed unto salvation and everlasting death in the Lake of Fire to those who rejected Christ as Savior.

Does it really make sense to think that punishment in the afterlife will bring those who have rejected God's love in the here and now to repentance? Our modern system of incarcerating people in "correctional institutions" certainly hasn't proven very successful at changing the hearts and attitudes of those locked up in them. And the Biblical example of God's chastening hand upon Israel never resulted in a universal turning back to God by His chosen people either.

If, as Universalism teaches, all people are the elect and predestined to salvation, then positionally all people are already "in Christ" and already have eternal life and are in no danger of being separated from God forever in Hell. They really have no need to be saved because they are safe and secure regardless of what they choose to believe about Christ. Having been guaranteed eternal life from before the foundation of the world, logically they have never really been lost, and the idea of ever being separated from God is only an illusion. If this were actually so, the Gospel of Jesus Christ as presented in the Bible would make no sense and would have no power to save anyone through faith because no one really has to trust in Christ to be saved.

A MOST IMPORTANT CONSIDERATION

Something that must be seriously considered when looking at the doctrine of Universalism is its ramifications. Universalists have no Scriptural proof whatsoever that anyone, let alone all, who die in their sins, will ever have an opportunity to believe the Gospel and be saved after they have suffered corrective punishment in Hell. The Bible is clear that at the Great White Throne Judgment all those who are not found written in the Book of Life will be *"cast into the Lake of Fire"* (Rev. 20:15). But, where does it say that finally they will be drawn out of the fire and awarded eternal life? Universalism says that they must be saved out of Hell even though they have no Scriptural evidence. Ignoring that He is also a God of perfect justice, all they can do is insist that a loving God would not send anyone to Hell forever because they do not think He would.

Our question here is, what if they are wrong? What will be the result of their teaching? If those who believe in an everlasting Hell are wrong, their error will not result in any lasting damage being done, as every human being will end up being saved anyway. But, on the other hand, if the Universalists are wrong, their error will result in many having a false hope that they will be saved regardless of what they believe. And since it does away with an absolute need for believers to take the Gospel Message to the regions beyond where people have not yet heard of Jesus Christ so they can be saved, it hinders mission work. Why go if you are not really needed? Rather than sacrificing to reach the lost, why not let them suffer for a time for their unbelief since they will finally be saved anyway? Especially since so many of them are hateful towards Christians and it can be dangerous to minister the Gospel Message in many places.

This teaching has the potential of influencing multitudes away from faith in Christ and hindering even more from ever hearing the Good News of salvation. This is a grave responsibility to take on based on anything other than a clear and undisputed passage of Scripture. The questionable hermeneutics of Universalism certainly do not offer anything that is substantial enough to risk the eternal destiny of lost souls on, but that is exactly what they are doing when they propagate this doctrine.

A LOOK AT UNIVERSALISM'S SCRIPTURAL EVIDENCE

While Universalism's proponents rely heavily on philosophical arguments to defend their beliefs, they also use the Bible to try to substantiate their beliefs.

Because they do appeal to the Scriptures to support their beliefs, it is important that we look at how they interpret the verses on which they attempt to build their doctrine.

THE MANY WHO WILL BE MADE RIGHTEOUS

Universalism says that Romans 5:19 teaches that as all men were made sinners in Adam so all men will also be made righteous in Christ. From this assumption, they conclude that all men will eventually believe and be saved, even if they die in their sins. But, in trying to

Universalism & Annihilationism

force this verse to fit their doctrine, they have ignored its context.

First, Paul's purpose in this passage is to explain to those who have been *"justified by faith"* (see Rom. 5:1) what it means to be in Christ in contrast to being in Adam. He sets this out in Romans 5:1-8:39. In other words, he is not dealing with who will be saved but with those who are already saved. Even so, we would have to at least acknowledge that the Universalist understanding might be a probable interpretation of Romans 5:19 except that Paul has inserted a qualifier into the passage. Let's look at what he has said in its context.

> *"And not as it was by one that sinned, so is the gift; for the judgment was by one to condemnation, but the free gift is of many offenses unto justification. For if by one man's offense death reigned by one; much more they which receive abundance of grace and the gift of righteousness shall reign in life by One; Jesus Christ. Therefore as by the offense of one judgment came upon all men to condemnation; even so by the righteousness of One the free gift came upon all men unto the justification of life. For as by one man's disobedience many were made sinners, so by the obedience of One shall many be made righteous"* (Rom. 5:16-19).

In verse 17, it is made clear that it is only those who *"receive...the gift of righteousness"* that *"shall reign in life."* The Greek word translated receive here is *lambano* and it is used in the present tense and active voice. So the content of this passage can only be applied to those Paul is addressing which are only those who have been

83

"justified by faith" and as a result *"have peace with God"* (Rom. 5:1). The overall context of the chapter disallows Universalism's interpretation of verse 19. Yes, Christ's blood is sufficient to save all of mankind, but it is only applied to those who receive the gift of eternal life that He has made available. Paul wrote to Timothy, *"For therefore we both labor and suffer reproach, because we trust in the Living God, who is the Savior of all men, specially of those who believe"* (I Tim. 4:10). Out of the *"all men"* that Christ died for, the salvation He made available is only applied to *"those who believe"* (also see I Cor. 1:18-21).

THE EVERLASTING LAKE OF FIRE

While the Scriptures are clear on the subject of the duration of the punishment of the wicked, Universalists deny that it will last forever and ever. Their argument from Scripture is based on the meaning of two Greek words, the noun *aion* and its adjective *aionios*. They insist that since the basic meaning of *aion* (or eon) is "age" that its meaning is limited to a specific period of time, or an age, and so the aionian punishment of the unsaved must be temporal in nature rather than being everlasting.

Because of the Universalist claims about the meaning of *aion* and *aionios*, it is important that we look at these words here. Vernon A. Schutz has written an excellent booklet on the subject entitled "Universal Reconciliation: Do the Eons Ever End?" which is subtitled "Does

Universalism & Annihilationism

Eon Ever Mean Eternal?" In this work, Pastor Schutz has challenged the premise of Universalism, which says that the phrases "for the age of the ages "(aion of the aions)" and "for the ages of the ages" (aions of the aions) have been incorrectly understood and thus wrongly translated as *"forever"* and *"ever"* in our English Bibles. In regards to how a word is used being vital to understanding its meaning he states:

> "It is the way the word is used in its context and circumstances that will determine whether or not aion means just an age or forever, or eternity. Aion in many New Testament passages obviously means just an age, such as Matthew 12:32: 'neither in this age, or in the age to come.' It would not make sense to say: 'neither in this eternity or the eternity to come.' It would be ridiculous to contend that eon or aion always means eternal or forever. However, it would be just as ridiculous to contend that aion never means eternal or forever but this is precisely the position of the U.R. (Universal Reconciliation: Do the Eons Ever End? Schutz, Vernon A., Grace Publications, Inc., Grand Rapids, MI 1978, pg. 5).

In reference to how the crowds would shout "the Emperor eis ton aiona (the Emperor forever)" in ancient times, Schutz goes on to say:

> Can anyone really feel or believe that the shout "The Emperor eis ton aiona" means, "The Emperor for an age?" Surely we can see that this meant "The Emperor forever." Therefore the context, the circumstances, and the usage of the word aion determines whether an age or eternity is in view. (Schutz, pg.6).

The primary principle of Bible interpretation is: Interpret in the light of context. This is important to keep in mind when looking at the Scriptures.

In his refutation of the Universalist claim that aion is never used to mean eternity, Schutz has aptly demonstrated that they are wrong through the parallelism of Hebrew poetry and its adaptation to the New Testament in the book of Luke. Hebrew poetry does not use rhyme or rhythm but employs a parallelism of ideas or thoughts. The following explanation and chart by Schutz makes this clear.

> In both Hebrew poetic and literary styles, the second of the two parallel statements often repeats, amplifies, or explains the first. For instance:
>
> The Lord of Hosts...is...with us:
> The God of Jacob...is...our refuge (Ps. 46:7).
> The law of the Lord...is...perfect restoring the soul;
> The testimony of the Lord...is...sure, making the wise the simple (Ps. 19:7).
>
> Both statements mean the same, but the second repeats the thought in different words. Observe Ps. 114:1.
>
> "When Israel...went out of...Egypt
> the House of Jacob...from...a people of strange language."
>
> It is obvious that the second line repeats the same thought of the first line. The same literary style is adhered to in Luke 1:33:

> "And He (Christ) shall reign over the
> House of Jacob...forever (eis tous aionas);
> and of His
> kingdom there shall be...no end (ouk telos)."
>
> The word forever is the Greek word eon or aion. Literally it is (eis tous aionas) or unto the ages. Notice the parallelisms: "The house of Jacob" is equivalent to or is the same as kingdom." "Unto the ages" is equivalent to or the same as "there shall be no end." (Schutz, pg. 7)

Schutz provides strong proof that aion can be, and is, used of that which will last forever, showing that Universalism is simply wrong in what they teach about its use. The combining of "parallelism" and "antithesis," a contrast or opposition of thought, is also found in Scripture. Schutz also shows how both Peter and Paul did this.

> Paul combines these two rules of language, paralleism and antithesis, in II Corinthians 4:17:
>
> *"For our light affliction, which is but for a moment, worketh for us a far more exceeding and eternal weight of glory."*
>
> Permit us to point out the parallelism and antithesis.
>
> our afflictions..........................light or insignificant
> our glory..................................weighty or great
> our afflictions....................momentary or temporal
> our glory..eternal or forever
>
> Peter does the same thing, only this time the noun eon is involved, and it has to mean endlessness or eternal.

The King James renders I Peter 1:23:

> *"Being born again, not of corruptible seed, but of incorruptible, by the word of God, which liveth and abideth forever."*

> The term forever is the translation of the Greek word eon or aion....one would think Peter would have used eon in the plural here and at least say that the Word abides for the ages. The very fact that Peter does not use the plural of eon shows us that aion in the singular had an idiomatic usage, that is, at times aion was used in the sense of forever, everlasting, or eternal.

> The parallelism and antithesis of this passage makes our point abundantly clear:

> Corruptible...seed...flesh...withereth...falleth away
> Incorruptible...Word...God...endureth...abides for ever

> (Schutz, pgs. 10-11)

Schutz' point is that those who say that the noun aion never means eternal are wrong. To say otherwise is to deny that *"the incorruptible"* Word of God *"abideth forever."* This is telling because if the singular of aion is used to convey the idea of that which is everlasting, as we have just seen that it is, then most surely when used in the plural form, the aions or the aions of the aions, it can and sometimes does mean everlasting or eternal.

We understand that these words can be used of an age (a certain period of time) or of unending time (eternity), depending on the context they are used in. And since aionios is used to describe God, who we know is by

Universalism & Annihilationism

nature an Eternal Being, it is again obvious that the word can be used to mean eternal or everlasting (see Rom. 16:26; I Tim. 6:16). In addition, the fact that the translators of the Septuagint used aionios to describe the eternal nature of God in Genesis 21:33 and Isaiah 40:28 shows that the word did indeed carry that meaning over 100 years before the New Testament was written. This proves that the meaning was not forced on it later by the translators as some Universalists (and Annihilationists) claim.

In the book of Matthew, we find the Lord Jesus pronouncing everlasting punishment on the wicked and ascribing eternal life to the righteous in the same verse. *"And these shall go away into everlasting* (aionios) *punishment: but the righteous into life eternal* (aionios)" (Mat. 25:46). The same Greek word, *aionios*, is used of both the punishment and the life given by the Lord here. Since the punishment of the lost is set in direct contrast to the blessing of the saved, the same duration of time must be assigned to both. In other words, if the life given by God to the believer is everlasting, so also will the punishment of God on the unbeliever be everlasting, as both are described by the same word in what is undeniably the same context and are set against each other as absolute opposites.

If both were treated equally, according to Universalists, we would have to say that the believers in this passage are only given "age-long life" just as the unbelievers are only assigned to an "age-long punishment."

The State and Place of the Dead

But, even if this were so, what happens at the end of the age would be opposite as well. If, in the aionion Kingdom, the sheep on the Lord's right hand are allowed to enter into their inheritance as only a prelude to their receiving of eternal life, then the aionion fire the goats on His left hand are cast into must be a prelude to the everlasting punishment that is their final destiny. In the context and manner aionios is used in these verses, the end results for both parties are graphically portrayed however one chooses to interpret it.

It is obvious that this proclamation of punishment stands in contrast to eternal life, which is the life of God that is given to the righteous. The unrighteous, on the other hand, will be separated from the life of God forever and ever. The same Greek words that are used to describe the eternal nature and God's worthiness to be praised and of eternal life are also used of the nature of the punishment of the wicked.

This is a dilemma for the Universalist. So, to get around this obvious contradiction to their doctrine, they resort to claiming that since we know that God is an Eternal Being, we can assign the meaning of eternal or everlasting to aion or aionios when they are used to describe Him or His works, but otherwise it never means that. However, that simply is not how language works. If a word or phrase can be used to describe something, even something unique, it can be used in the same way to describe other things. They acknowledge

Universalism & Annihilationism

that these words are often used in regard to eternal life, but when used of the punishment of the wicked the Universalist says it has to be temporary based on their presupposition that Hell cannot be everlasting. In other words, they interpret the word according to what they have decided to believe and simply ignore the context it is found in along with the normal principles of hermeneutics. Just because we want something to be true does not make it true, regardless of any effort to force an interpretation of Scripture that agrees with one's preferences. Besides, if the aionios life given can be deemed eternal because it was given by the eternal God, then the aionios punishment must also be seen as eternal for the same reason.

In dealing with this passage, they also point to the Greek word for punishment, *kolasis*, saying that it can only refer to a remedial or corrective type punishment because the word carries the idea of "cutting off" or "pruning." But, that is not an accurate assessment as it is found in other Greek literature in reference to divine punishment. Regardless though, as we have already said, since it is set as the opposite of eternal life, the punishment in view must be everlasting in nature as well or the obvious contrast is made meaningless. Even so, the idea of pruning or cutting off does not negate the concept of everlasting punishment because the penalty of sin is death, which speaks of being "separated" or "cutoff" from the presence of the Lord. To know God is eternal life (Jn. 17:3), to not know Him then is eternal destruction from His presence (II Thes. 1:9). Whatever kind of punishment the unrighteous will suffer, it will last as long as the life given to the righteous. This verse by itself renders Universalism an untenable doctrine. And, when we look at where the unrighteous are being sent to be punished, we see that it is a place of *"everlasting fire"* that was originally created as a place of punishment for Satan and the fallen angels (Mat. 25:41).

If Universalism is true and the punishment of the Lake of Fire is only temporary and remedial, then logically the Devil and his demons would have to be purified and made righteous in Hell as well. Actually some Universalists do teach this, but there is no Scriptural evidence of any such hope for Satan and the fallen angels or for mankind.

THE BOWING OF EVERY KNEE

Universalists look at Philippians 2:10 and say that the fact that eventually *"every knee should bow"* at the name of Jesus Christ proves that all of mankind will eventually be saved. But, based on their presuppositions about the fate of those who die in their sins, they read much more into this verse than is there. To bow down before someone does not necessarily have to be an act of adoration and worship as would be expected of believers who come into the presence of Jesus Christ. It can also be done in an act of acknowledgment and submission. When those who have died in their sins are

Universalism & Annihilationism

brought before the Great White Throne to be judged for their works (see Rev. 20:11-13), they will no doubt fall down before the Holy One who is sitting on the throne as their Judge. The God they rejected in favor of His creation will be acknowledged as their Creator and the Sovereign of the universe while bowing to Him as vanquished foes.

Yes, *"every knee should bow"* to the Exalted One and *"every tongue should confess that Jesus Christ is Lord"* (see Phil. 2:9-11), but only the redeemed will do it in joy and adoration of the One who is worthy of praise. The lost, on the other hand, will do so in shame and despair. Their defiant hearts laid bare (Heb. 12-13; Jer. 17:9-10), they will acknowledge that they are worthy only of the righteous judgment pronounced on them and will not offer any defense or speak a word of protest against their deserved fate (Rom. 1:18-20, 32; 3:19).

THE NATURE OF THE KINGDOM AND THE LAKE OF FIRE

The Millennial Kingdom is connected to eternity in the sense that even though it will give way to the eternal state at the end of the 1,000 year reign of Jesus Christ on earth, His rule will continue unabated from one age to the other.

When the Lord Jesus returns to earth to claim the throne of David that is rightfully His, *"Of the increase of His government and peace there shall be no end, upon His throne of David, and upon His kingdom, to order it, and to establish it with judgment and justice from*

henceforth even forever. The zeal of the Lord of Hosts will perform this" (Isa. 9:7; cf. Dan. 2:44; 7:13-14; Lk. 1:32-33; II Pet. 1:11; Rev. 11:15).

In contrast to the blessings of Christ's eternal Kingdom, Hell, or the Lake of Fire, is a place of personal and everlasting separation from the presence of God (II Thes. 1:8-10; Mat. 7:23; 8:12; 25:32; Rev. 14:10-11; 21:8).

As we pointed out earlier, Universalism tries to deny the everlastingness of the torment of the Lake of Fire by saying the term used to describe it has been mistranslated. They claim that since the Greek literally says "ages of the ages" (Rev. 14:11; 20:10), it only refers to an "age-long" or "age-lasting fire" of limited duration. They do this in spite of the evidence that the Bible writers expressed the idea of eternity with this term. As we have already looked at the translation issue and word meanings, what we want to look at here is how the meaning that Universalism gives to aion and aionios would actually affect the length of time that those who are cast into the Lake of Fire will be there.

All of the unsaved will be consigned to the Lake of Fire either at the beginning of the Millennial Kingdom (Mat. 25:41,46; Rev. 19:20) or at the end of it (Rev. 20:7-15). For any of them to remain in the Lake of Fire until the *"ages of the ages"* comes to an end must mean that they will have to wait until multiple ages have ended. That would be at least four different ages as that would be the minimum number that the double plurality of the ages of the ages could refer to. Of course, since the Eternal Kingdom that follows the Millennial Kingdom age will never come to an end, those who end up in the Lake of Fire would be there forever and ever, wouldn't they? If the idea of ages of the ages is not that of long ages followed by ages upon ages to represent that which never ends, then it must refer to multiple ages that succeed each other until the last one comes to an end. No such ages upon ages that follow the Millennium can be identified in the Scriptures as they only exist in the imagination of the Universalists.

THINGS TO THINK ABOUT IN REGARDS TO UNIVERSALISM

Most of those born and raised in the Kingdom, after living under Christ's reign of righteousness, will rebel against Him at the end of the thousand years (Rev. 20:7-10). Is it reasonable then to think that their hearts will be changed by the "remedial fires" of Hell as Universalism claims? We don't think so and, when we look at the overall picture of judgment found in the Bible, we do not find the idea of those who die in their sins finally being saved. Consider the following:

1. Does the cursed fig tree of Mark 11:12-14 picture universal salvation?

2. As the price for sin is death, and sin is a transgression of God's eternal character, how long would it take for those delivered to the tormentors to pay their sin debt? Mat. 18:34-35; cf. 25:28-30.

3. Does being cut off from Israel and being forever banished from the Promised Land picture the idea of Universalism or everlasting punishment? Ex. 12:15; 31:14; Lev. 7:20-21; Num. 15:30.

4. When the Lord banishes sinners from His Kingdom, does He offer any hope for their eternal return? Mat. 7:13-27; 8:10-12; 22:1-14; 25:41,46.

5. What is the picture painted by the prophet Isaiah of the differences between those who will enter the New Heavens and New Earth and those who won't in Isaiah chapter 65?

6. Who are the only ones allowed to enter the New Jerusalem? Where are those who are not allowed in? Rev. 20:15 with 21:4.

7. What are the various ways that unbelievers are pictured in regards to punishment in the following verses? Mat. 3:7-12; 7:13; 25:30,41,46; Lk. 16:22-24; Jn. 3:36; I Cor. 1:18; Heb. 10:27; II Pet. 2:12,17; 3:7.

8. What does it mean that *"there remaineth no more sacrifice for sins"* for those who willfully rebel against the truth? Heb. 10:26; cf. Heb. 6:4-6.

9. If the terrible judgment of the Tribulation won't turn the masses of humanity to Christ, why should we think that being consigned to the Lake of Fire will? Rev. 6:14-17; 16:4-11.

10. Would not a salvation that is accomplished though an individual being justly punished for his sinful deeds be antithetical to the grace of God? Rev. 20:11-15.

Universalism & Annihilationism

11. If the righteous (believers) are "barely saved," what will be the lot of ungodly sinners *"that obey not the Gospel of God"*? I Pet. 4:17-18; cf. Prov. 11:29-31.

12. As only the redeemed will be allowed to enter into the Millennial Kingdom, and entrance into it denotes being in God's presence and the receiving of eternal life, is it not so then, that being denied entrance has been set in contrast to those who are allowed in to indicate everlasting judgment and separation from God? Mat. 7:13-27; 25:34,41,46.

13. What is the significance of the Lord Jesus' warning to the scribes and Pharisees that if they persisted in their unbelief they would die in their sins (Jn. 8:21-24)? Isn't this essentially the same thing that John the Baptist was proclaiming when he said, *"He that believeth on the Son hath everlasting life: and he that believeth not the Son shall not see life; but he wrath of God abideth on Him"* (Jn. 3:36)? Comparing these passages in their contexts (Jn. 3:1-36 & 8:12-27), doesn't it seem obvious that the only opportunity offered to believe in the Son in these passages is before physical death? Isn't the intended contrast obvious that those who die in unbelief will be forever cut off from the life of God to suffer His wrath while those who die in faith will have everlasting life?

14. Why was Paul so burdened over the unbelieving Jews that he was willing to be *"accursed from Christ"* if it would result in their salvation (Rom. 9:1-3; 10:1), if in truth they will all individually be saved in the end anyway?

THE DOCTRINE OF ANNIHILATIONISM

Those who believe in Annihilationism hold the same or similar views about the meaning and use of the word aion as Universalists do. Obviously, they must deny that it means eternal or they would have no argument against everlasting punishment at all. In addition, they must also hold to the position that the soul of man does not exist in a conscious state of being between the time of physical death and resurrection. The state of man between death and resurrection, according to this view, has been referred to as soul sleep, the dissolution of the soul, or the eradication of the soul. There may also be other terminology that we are not aware of that is used by some. Regardless of what it is called though, it is all done in an effort to deny the immortality of the soul of the human being. They must disprove the fact that once a human being comes into existence as a person they will exist forever or else the Doctrine of Annihilationism is annihilated. So, they go to great lengths to do so. Much effort on their part has been put into trying to make the account of the Rich Man and Lazarus (Luke 16:19-31) say something other than what it says because it clearly teaches that humans continue to exist in a conscious state of being after physical death. Special effort is put into this because if left to its normal meaning as written this passage of Scripture leaves no room for the doctrine of Annihilationism.

Universalism & Annihilationism

As we have already dealt with the immortality of the human soul under the section entitled the "Intermediate State" we will not revisit it here. There are, however several different views among those who deny the immortality of the soul. One view that is similar to Annihilationism is the idea of <u>Conditional Immortality</u>. Pastor C.R. Stam gives a brief explanation of the variations in the beliefs associated with these views.

> "In the camp of those who hold that the ungodly will finally cease to exist there are wide differences of opinion. Most of those who hold to Conditional Immortality, believe that man, being mortal, is destined, in the nature of the case, to pass out of existence and that only through union with Christ can he obtain so-called 'immortality.' Those who hold to Annihilation, on the other hand, believe that the ungodly will be exterminated or put out of existence. This, however, is only a very general distinction for, as we say, the differences of opinion in this school of thought are many and great.
>
> Some believe that there will be a single act of annihilation, others a process of destruction; some, that it will be a punishment, others, a merciful deliverance from punishment; some, that the ungodly cease to exist at the first death, others, that this does not take place until the second death. But these last are disagreed again as to whether the second death will annihilate its victims immediately or sooner or later after sufficient punishment. Again, some believe that in the case of the unsaved, man as such will cease to exist at death but will be brought into existence again to be tried and destroyed in the second death, while others hold that

since (according to their theory) the ungodly cease to exist at death there can be no resurrection for them. Still others hold that "the soul survives the death of the body until judgment day, when God will destroy both soul and body of the wicked in the lake of fire.'" (Man, His Nature and Destiny, by Cornelius R. Stam, Berean Bible Society, 1961, pgs. 194-195 emphasis in original).

None of these views have any Biblical basis on which to stand even though their proponents have vigorously tried to defend them with certain proof texts that they claim prove their doctrine. Speaking of both Universalism and Annihilationism, C.R. Stam explains where they have erred.

> "Both deny conscious existence in death. Both deny the accepted meaning of those terms rendered 'everlasting' and 'forever and ever' in the Authorized Version. Both argue that God would be unjust to punish the wicked forever. But neither has concluded from the Scriptures that everlasting punishment is not taught here. They have concluded this from their own reasoning and then have sought to prove their conclusions from certain Scriptures. In doing so, however, they have been forced to ignore the Holy Spirit's usage of the terms in question and to pervert the plainest statements of the Word of God. (Stam, pg. 194)."

We agree with Pastor Stam's assessment of these dangerous doctrines and pray that the Lord will deliver those who have been deceived by them from this snare of the Devil in which they have been caught (II Tim. 2:24-26). But, before leaving this subject we think that it is important that we look at some of the arguments of the Annihilationists.

MAN IS ONLY TWO PARTS

Appealing to Genesis 2:7, which says of Adam that God *"breathed into his nostrils the breath of life; and man became a living soul"* some claim that man is only a two part being made up of a body and a spirit, with the soul being made up of the two. In other words, the conscious part of man, the soul, only exists while the body and spirit of man are in union. When the body dies the soul dies with it and when the spirit is separated from the body the soul simply ceases to exist according to this view. However, this is not what the Bible teaches. In His commission address to the twelve men called as apostles, the Lord Jesus told them that they had no need to fear other men as they could only *"kill the body, but are not able to kill the soul"* (Mat. 10:28). If, in fact, the soul of a man dies when his body does then this straight forward statement of the Lord Jesus Christ to His disciples would be a lie. By putting another person to death physically a murderer would be killing that person's soul as well. According to the Lord Jesus Christ this is simply not possible. Following are further thoughts on why this two-part view of man and the death of the soul is Scripturally unsound.

The words soul and spirit are sometimes used in Scripture in what seems to be an interchangeable manner in reference to the inner man. This is because the soul and spirit are both immaterial in nature and the two are intricately tied together. But, there is a difference between them. In Scripture they are clearly shown to be two different parts of that which makes up the whole man. In his first letter to the Thessalonians, the Apostle Paul shows that man consists of three parts when it says; *"And the very God of peace sanctify you wholly; and I pray God your whole spirit and soul and body be preserved blameless unto the coming of our Lord Jesus Christ"* (I Thes. 5:23).

This passage would make no sense if the soul was only the result of the union of the spirit and the body. To preserve only the spirit and body would be to make sure that the soul would be found blameless if the soul is only a result of the two being brought together. Also, if this dichotomous (two-part) teaching were true, then the body would necessarily have to be considered as part of the essence of the life of man rather than as the tabernacle or dwelling place that the Scriptures say that it is (see II Cor. 4:7; 5:1-4; II Pet. 1:13-14). As a dwelling place, or tent of temporary residence, it is not a part of the soul and the soul does not depend on it to exist. If it did, it would mean that a believer's body would have to be renewed along with their spirit when they trust in Christ for the forgiveness of sins and are regenerated.

The believer is saved by grace through faith apart from works and *"made alive together with Christ"* (Eph. 2:4-5, 8-9). At that time, the believer experiences *"the washing of regeneration of the Holy Spirit which is shed* (poured out) *on us abundantly through Jesus Christ our Savior"* (Titus 3:5-6) and is made *"complete in Him"* (Col. 2:9-10). Yes, there remains the promise of resurrection when the believer will receive a glorified body because that is part of the redemption package. But, the Scriptures make it clear that the person, the individual soul which is the essence of our conscious being, is already totally justified and reconciled to God through the redemption that is in Christ Jesus our Lord when they believe (Rom. 3:24; 5:10-11). The believer's soul salvation is spoken of as something that is a present possession *"we have redemption through His blood,"* (Eph. 1:7) and as having taken place in the past *"according to His mercy He saved us,"* (Titus 3:5).

On the other hand, the physical part of the believer, the body, is said to still be awaiting total redemption; *"we ourselves groan within ourselves, waiting for the adoption, to wit, the redemption of the body,"* (Rom. 8:23; cf. I Cor. 15:1-4, 19-23; II Cor. 4:13-14 with Eph. 1:13-14; I Thes. 4:13-18).

Now, our point is that if the very existence of the soul of man depends on the physical life of the body, as those who believe in the extinction of the soul at the time of physical death maintain, how can believers be said to be justified and complete in Christ if the body is not yet regenerated? If the soul only exists when the body is alive then the body must be an essential part of the soul just as the spirit is. It can only follow then, that for the soul to be redeemed, both the body and spirit must be redeemed. This goes against the testimony of Scripture that teaches that the individuals' soul is spiritually renewed at the time of salvation but must wait until sometime in the future before his or her body is renewed. Thus, as a redeemed entity, the souls of departed believers do, and must, remain alive in a conscious state of being from the time of physical death until the Rapture because they are spiritually alive.

Another point that must be made on this subject is that of the sealing by the Holy Spirit of believers. If the conscious part of a believer, that is the soul, or the person, ceases to exist, the Holy Spirit, who the Bible says regenerates and indwells all believers and seals them until the day of redemption, would have nothing to indwell or to seal. The teaching of the Bible is that the indwelling of the Holy Spirit provides and maintains the believer's spiritual life and gives absolute assurance of the hope of a future resurrection. Since the believer is sealed in Christ until that day, the believer will remain in a conscious state of existence until that day. To say otherwise is to make the Bible's testimony of the unconditional and continuing completeness of the believer's salvation and sealing of the Holy Spirit meaningless. We believe that man is body, soul, and spirit and that the soul of man survives the death of the body as a spiritual entity in a conscious state of being.

The saved go to be with the Lord while awaiting their resurrection unto glory, and the unsaved go to Sheol/Hades to wait for their resurrection unto condemnation.

THE DIVINE SATIRE THEORY OF LUKE 16:19-31

Because the story of the Rich Man and Lazarus in Luke 16 refutes the idea of annihilation, Annihilationists deny that the account teaches any truth about the conscious state of the dead between physical death and resurrection. Some have resorted to the idea of it being a "divine satire" saying that Christ was simply using a misbelief of the Pharisees to teach them truth. They say that by using Jewish fables about angels transporting the souls of the dead to their final place of abode, the Lord was only making the point that even if one rose from the dead to warn them the Pharisees would not believe, since they did not believe the Scriptures in the first place. Those who hold to this or a similar view usually say that the Rich Man represents the nation of Israel while Lazarus, the beggar, represents the Gentiles. The account must be seen as a parable or an allegory according to this view. We believe that this is an erroneous interpretation that is forced on the passage by the use of faulty hermeneutics and unsound doctrine.

To say that the Rich Man and Lazarus respectively represent national Israel and the Gentiles rather than individuals simply does not fit the facts. It is said, by those holding this view, that the Rich Man's blessings of clothes of purple and fine linen and luxurious living pictures the blessings of God on Israel and that the poor beggar Lazarus represents the needy Gentiles. The point being that the Gentiles would come into the blessings that Israel was on the verge of losing. Historically, prophetically, and dispensationally this is an impossible interpretation of Luke 16:19-31.

It is historically impossible because it simply does not fit the facts of Israel's history. Yes, Israel was promised blessings from God but, under the Law of Moses, they could only partake of them when in obedience to God. Throughout their history as a nation, Israel only periodically tasted those blessings. For the most part, they had been under chastisement by the Lord because of their backsliding ways. The historical fact is that, at the time of Jesus Christ's earthly ministry, Israel had for the most part been dispersed among the nations and had been under Gentile rule for almost 600 years. The ruling Gentiles had *"fared sumptuously,"* while Israel was the beggar nation. At this point in history it was Rome that was *"clothed in purple and fine linen,"* as were the Greeks, the Persians, and the Babylonians before them. On and off before and continually since the destruction of Jerusalem in 586 B.C., Israel as a whole has been in need. Both spiritually and materially! It is important to take note here that a constant theme throughout the prophets and the Gospel Records is the rebuke and warning of judgment on the rich and powerful of Israel

Universalism & Annihilationism

for how they treated their own people who were in need. This is exactly what we find in the story of the Rich Man and Lazarus who obviously were both Jews.

This view is prophetically impossible because it pictures the Gentiles receiving God's blessings at the expense of Israel. According to prophecy, the opposite is true as the Gentiles are to be blessed through believing Israel. Prophetically, it will not be until Israel receives the fullness of her blessings in the Millennial Kingdom that the Gentiles will be able to eat the scraps from the children's table (Mk. 7:24-30; cf. Isa. 49:5-6, 22-23; 60:1-3; 61:5-6; 62:1-2). Until that time Israel will continue to be the *"tail"* nation (Deut. 28:44). This is a foundational truth of God's prophetic program for Israel and the nations of the world.

Dispensationally, this interpretation is impossible even though Gentiles are today partakers of Israel's spiritual blessings (Rom. 15:27) through the Gospel of Grace given to the Apostle Paul (Rom. 15:16; cf. Rom. 11:13; Gal. 1:11-12; etc.). Jesus Christ's earthly ministry was to the "circumcision" (Israel) *"for the truth of God, to confirm the promises made unto the fathers"* (Rom. 15:8). His message for that time was prophetic in nature, confirming that God's promises of material and spiritual blessings to Israel's forefathers will indeed be fulfilled when the kingdom of David is restored after Messiah returns in power and glory, a kingdom in which Israel will be at the head of the nations. But, in the present dispensation, the message that the Lord gave to Paul when He appointed him the Apostle of the Gentiles does not recognize Israel's advantage as God's chosen nation and offers no guarantee of physical blessings to anyone as the Kingdom Gospel does. It is an unprophecied, or secret, program that makes no distinction between Jews and Gentiles. Thus we see that the interpretation that the Rich Man represents Israel and the beggar the Gentiles does not, and cannot fit, into the parameters of the Dispensation of Grace just as it does not fit the facts of history or the proclamation of prophecy.

THE PLACEMENT OF THE COMMA IN LUKE 23:43

Annihilationists do not accept Luke 23:43 as written in the Bible because it refutes their position. The Lord Jesus' words to the repentant thief were, *"Verily I say unto thee, today shalt thou be with Me in paradise."* Not willing to accept that the thief went into Hades in a conscious state of being with Christ when he died, the claim is made that the comma found after *"Verily I say unto thee,...."* should be moved to after *"today,"* rendering the passage *"Verily I say unto thee today,...."* They say that the Lord Jesus was simply promising on the day they died that at some time in the future the thief would join Him in Paradise. With this understanding, this verse could be paraphrased as follows, "Today I am telling you the truth, eventually you will be with me in

Universalism & Annihilationism

paradise." In support of this idea they teach that Moses' use of *"this day"* in Deuteronomy is a common Hebrew idiom that should be carried over in our understanding of Luke 23:43. This is seriously flawed.

Moses' use of the term *"this day"* in Deuteronomy is more than the employment of a common idiom of his day. It is found 42 times in the book, which is significant because of the content of Moses' message to Israel in Deuteronomy. Moses used heaven and earth as his witnesses against Israel as he restated the Law and the terms of Israel's covenant with God, reminding a new generation that it was as binding on them as it had been on their forefathers (see Deut. 4:26; 30:19-20). It was a new day for Israel as they were preparing to enter the Promised Land, and the use of the term *"this day"* was not simply an idiom used for emphasis but as a direct reference to the time of Moses' final charge to Israel. They would have no excuse for disobedience as God's commandments were not hidden but were written down for all to read. This fact was established on the day Moses proclaimed it to them (see Deut. 30:10-20). Isaiah reminded the nation of this when he called upon heaven and earth to listen as he pronounced God's judgment on Israel as a rebellious people (Isa. 1:2-5). It had a distinct purpose for the time and circumstances in which Moses used it, so it cannot simply be transferred forward 1500 years and claimed as a common idiom of the time of Christ.

Also, there is no evidence in the Gospel Records of Christ's life that He ever used *"this day"* as an idiom as its proponents claim He did in Luke 23:43. However, we do find several examples of the term *"this day"* used in reference to events to come soon just as He did in Luke 23 (see Mk. 14:30; Lk. 2:11; 4:21; 5:26; 12:28; 13:32-33; 19:5,9; 22:34; 24:21). Both the textual and the internal evidence is overwhelmingly strong for the normal understanding of Luke 23:43; *"And Jesus said unto him, Verily I say unto thee, Today shalt thou be with me in Paradise."*

ABSENT FROM THE BODY

The Apostle Paul's statement, *"we are confident, I say, and willing rather to be absent from the body, and to be present with the Lord"* (II Cor. 5:8) has been explained away by saying that Paul only meant that he had a desire to be absent from his body and present with the Lord, but he realized that could only take place later in the resurrection. Yes, it is true that the eventual resurrection and glorification of believers is the primary subject of the overall context where this verse is found (II Cor. 4:7-5:10). However, this does not mean that verse eight does not mean exactly what it says. When a believer departs from their *"earthly house"* or *"tabernacle"* (II Cor. 5:1) at the time of physical death, he becomes *"absent from the body"* and immediately goes *"to be present with the Lord."* The point Paul is making is that every believer should have a desire to receive their resurrection body (II Cor. 5:1-4). He also makes it clear that our confidence that God will provide such a body for every believer should not waiver because He *"hath given unto us the earnest* (literally-down payment as a guarantee) *of the spirit"* (II Cor. 5:5; cf. Rom. 8:23; II Cor. 1:21-22; Eph. 1:13-14; 4:30). His conclusion is *"Therefore we are always confident, knowing that, while we are at home in the body, we are absent from the Lord: (for we walk by faith, not by sight:) we are confident I say, and willing rather to be absent from the body, and to be present with the Lord"* (II Cor. 5:6-8).

In other words, trusting in the testimony of God's Word, the saint is to walk in the confidence of faith, knowing that no matter what happens he or she will one day receive a glorified resurrection body. Their hope should be to experience the Rapture but, if the Lord tarries, they should not fear death but be willing to depart from the body if necessary, because they know that when they do they will go directly into the presence of the Lord.

We should point out that the death that is in view here is martyrdom (see II Cor. 4:7-12). Paul well knew what it was to suffer persecution for the Gospel of Christ. He also knew that regardless of the amount of suffering one might experience in this life on behalf of Christ, it is nothing when compared to the glory that lies ahead (II Cor. 4:15-17; cf. Rom. 8:17-25). Even if it means dying for the sake of the Gospel (see II Tim. 4:6-8), we need not let our troubles push us to the point of distress, anxiousness, or despair (II Cor. 4:8). No matter how harsh persecution might become, the Lord will not abandon us. Even if we are struck down and killed, we cannot be destroyed (II Cor. 4:9). Death has not yet been vanquished in that it still claims the physical part of man, the body. But, it cannot, nor can any other thing, separate the believer *"from the love of God, which is in Christ Jesus our Lord"* (Rom. 8:38-39). The soul of the believer is not destroyed at the time of physical death as those who believe that it is eradicated would have us believe. *"To be absent from the body" is indeed to be "present with the Lord."* We know that this is true because the Bible tells us so!

PAUL'S DESIRE TO DEPART AND BE WITH CHRIST

In Philippians 1:23, the Apostle Paul expressed his desire to depart this life to be with the Lord Jesus, which he knew would be *"far better"* than staying here. In order to get around the teaching of this verse, soul sleep and soul eradication proponents are forced to change its meaning. They claim it really means that Paul only had a strong desire that Christ would return so that he could be with Him. They try to substantiate their interpretation and re-translation of this verse through a word study of the Greek word *analuo*, which is translated *"depart"* in this verse. This word is only found twice in the Bible, here in Philippians and in Luke 12:36, where it is rendered *"return."* The argument is that it should be translated *"return"* in both places. The various Greek lexicons we checked with all basically say the same thing, that the word means to "loose" or "undo" as in setting a ship loose from its mooring lines. All but one gave both depart and return as valid renderings. Molton's "Analytical Greek Lexicon Revised" favored "to depart" for both places it is found. This means, like good Bereans, we have to determine from the context how the word is used, and thus its meaning, in the verse it is found in.

When we consider the subject matter of Philippians 1:19-26, it is apparent that what the Apostle had in mind was his desire "to be loosed" from his body so he could be with Christ. In verses 12-18, he explains that his being in prison had actually furthered the Gospel rather then hinder it. He also expressed his joy over others who were preaching Christ, regardless of their motivations.

In verse 19 Paul expresses his confidence that God would deliver him from prison, in answer to the prayers of the Philippians, through the power of the Holy Spirit.

In verse 20 his heart's desire is that he will have a good testimony in order to magnify Jesus Christ in all that he would do in this life or in death.

In verse 21 *"For to me to live is Christ, and to die is gain."* This is the key verse of the passage. *"To live is*

Christ": Paul is speaking here of his opportunity in this life to serve and glorify Jesus Christ and of the personal vibrant relationship he had with the Lord. *"To die is gain"* explains why he was as willing to magnify Christ in death as he was in life. As good and as fulfilling as life is in the service of the Lord, to die and enter into His personal presence is better. The only thing that can make a life that is *"in Christ"* better is to add more of Christ.

Verses 22-23 must be looked at together to grasp the full meaning of the Apostle's *"desire to depart and to be with Christ."* This was something that he said was far better for him than his other choice, which was to live on in the flesh of his body in order to take the opportunity of producing spiritual fruit (v.22). Notice that he had a choice in this matter and was torn between the two options. He could stay and magnify Christ through his life, which would produce fruit (spiritual profit) through his labors. Or he could go directly to be with the Lord Himself, which was not just better, but would be *"far better."* This had nothing to do with any idea on Paul's part that the eradication of his soul through physical death would be *"gain"* or better, than living on in prison as is claimed by some. He had already said that being in prison was "good" as Christ was magnified through it. Besides, he was not living in a prison cell but in his own hired house where people came to him to hear the Word of God preached (Acts 28:30-31). There can be

Universalism & Annihilationism

little doubt that, as far as his physical situation was concerned, he was probably more comfortable there than he had been anywhere else that he had ministered over the years (see II Cor. 11:22-33 and Acts chapters 9-28). Yes, Paul had a desire for the Lord to come for the Church, but that is not the desire expressed here. The time of the Rapture is strictly God's choice but, as we have already pointed out, Paul potentially had a choice in this matter. He knew full well that, when he stood before Caesar, if he needlessly antagonized the emperor, he would be put to death. On the other hand, he could simply share the Grace of God in Christ with him, as he had done with other government authorities, and trust that the Lord would deliver him, which Paul was confident He would do.

In verses 24-26 Paul makes the unselfish choice by deciding to *"abide in the flesh"* because of the spiritual need of the Philippians (and the Church in general, no doubt), for the furtherance of their joy and faith that their rejoicing may be *"more abundant in Jesus Christ."*

WISE WORDS FROM THE PAST

As we bring our look at Universalism and Annihilationism to a close, we would like to point the reader to John 3:36 as a verse to ponder: *"He that believeth on the Son hath everlasting life: and he that believeth not the Son shall not see life; but the wrath of God abideth on him."* We hope that you will think about this verse and consider the words of a letter written by C.H. Macintosh to a friend about 150 years ago:

"Beloved friend,

I have been thinking a good deal of late, on the last verse of the third chapter of John. It seems to me to furnish a most powerful answer to two of the leading heresies of this our day, namely Universalism on the one hand and Annihilationism, on the other: "He that believeth on the Son hath everlasting life; and he that believeth not the Son, shall not see life; but the wrath of God abideth on him."

The deniers of eternal punishment, as you know, are divided into two classes, differing from each other very materially. The one professes to believe that all will ultimately be restored and brought into everlasting felicity; these are the Universalists. The other is of the opinion that all who die out of Christ are annihilated, soul and body-made an end of thoroughly-will perish like the beast.

I think you will agree with me that John iii.36 completely demolishes both these fatal errors. It meets the Universalist by the sweeping and conclusive statement that the unbeliever "shall not see life." It entirely sets aside the notion of all being restored and eternally saved. Those who refuse to believe the Son shall die in their sins and never see life.

But, were this all, the Annihilationist might say, "Exactly so; that is just what I believe. None but those who believe in the Son shall live eternally. Eternal life is only in the Son, and hence, all who die out of Christ shall perish soul and body shall be made an end of."

Universalism & Annihilationism

Not so, says the Holy Spirit. It is quite true they shall not see life; but tremendous fact! "The wrath of God abideth on him." This beyond all question, gives a flat contradiction to annihilationism. If the wrath of God is to abide upon the unbeliever, it is utterly impossible he can be made an end of. Annihilation and abiding wrath are wholly incompatible. We must either erase the word "abiding" from the inspired page, or abandon completely the notion of annihilation. To hold the two is out of the question.

Of course, I am merely now referring to this one passage of Holy Scripture; and truly it is enough of itself to settle any mind that simply bows to the voice of God, as to the solemn question of eternal punishment. But, beloved friend, here is just the point. Men will not submit to the teaching and authority of Holy Scripture. They presume to sit in judgment upon what is and what is not worthy of God to do. They imagine that people may live in sin, in folly, in rebellion against God, and in the neglect of His Christ, and after all go unpunished. They take upon them to decide that it is inconsistent with their idea of God to allow such a thing as eternal punishment. They attribute to the government of God what we should consider a weakness in any human government, namely, an inability to punish evil-doers.

But ah! The Word of God is against them. It speaks of "unquenchable fire" of an "undying worm" of a "fixed gulf" of "abiding wrath." What, I would ask, is the meaning of such words, in the judgment of any honest, unprejudiced mind? It may be said that these are figures. Granted that the "fire," the "worm" and the "gulf" are figures, but figures of what? Of something ephemeral something which must, sooner of later, have an end? Nay; but something which is eternal, if anything is eternal.

If we deny eternal punishment, we must deny an eternal anything, inasmuch as it is the same word which is used in every instance to express the idea of endless continuance. There are about seventy passages in the Greek New Testament where the word "everlasting" occurs. It is applied, amongst many other things, to the life which believers possess, and to the punishment of the wicked, as in Matthew xxv. 46. Now, upon what principle can anyone attempt to take out the six or seven passages in which it applies to the punishment of the wicked, and say that in all these instances it does not mean for ever; but that in all the rest it does? I confess this seems to be perfectly unanswerable. If the Holy Ghost, if the Lord Jesus Christ Himself had thought proper to make use of a different word, when speaking in punishment of the wicked, from what He uses when speaking of the life of believers, I grant there might be some basis for an objection.

But no; we find the same word invariably used to express what everybody knows to be endless; and therefore if the punishment of the wicked be not endless, nothing is endless. They cannot, consistently, stop short with the question of punishment, but must go on to the denial of the very existence of God Himself.

Indeed, I cannot but believe that here lies the real root of the matter. The enemy desires to get rid of the word of God, of the Spirit of God, the Christ of God, and God Himself; and he craftily begins by introducing the thin end of his fatal wedge, in the denial of eternal punishment; and when this is admitted, the soul has taken the first step on the inclined plane which leads down to the dark abyss of atheism.

This may seem strong, harsh, and ultra; but it is my deep and thorough conviction; and I feel most solemnly impressed with the necessity of warning all our young friends against the danger of admitting into their minds the very shadow of a question or doubt as to the divinely established truth of the endless punishment of the wicked in hell. The unbeliever cannot be restored, for Scripture declares "he shall not see life." Moreover, he cannot be annihilated, for Scripture declares that "the wrath of God abideth upon him."

O my beloved friend, how much better and wiser and safer it would be for our fellow men to flee from the wrath to come than to deny that it is coming; or that, when it does come, it will be eternal.

Believe me, Most affectionately yours,

C.H.M"

(From the "Miscellaneous Writings of C.H.M.", Loizeaux Brothers, New York, NY, Vol. V, pgs. 174-178.)

"For the preaching of the cross is to them that perish foolishness; but unto us which are saved it is the power of God." (I Cor. 1:18).

The State and Place of the Dead

5

Conclusion

The Scriptural evidence for the existence of an everlasting place of separation and punishment called the Lake of Fire and that those who are assigned there will suffer endless torment is overwhelmingly strong. Based on the teachings of Scripture, the doctrines of Universalism and Annihilationism must both be rejected as false and dangerous. The same is true of any belief that denies that individuals continue to exist in a conscious state of being between physical death and resurrection. Only by placing personal faith in Jesus Christ and His finished work of redemption can anyone escape being sentenced to the Lake of Fire forever. Behold, now is the day of salvation and it is only by trusting in Christ before death that a person can be forgiven of their sins and be redeemed. Believe on the Lord Jesus Christ, and you will be saved.

Appendix

Further Considerations

In addition to what we have already covered on the subjects of Universalism and Annihilationism we would like to make available to the reader some material that we put together while doing research in preparation for writing on these doctrines. We did the research in these areas in response to some of the statements that we found in the writings of the prominent proponents of Universalism and Annihilationism. We felt that incorporating this material into the main body of the article would make it too cumbersome, but at the same time realized that some would appreciate having this information available. We hope that it will be found helpful by those who are interested.

THE INFLUENCE OF MARVIN VINCENT

Marvin R. Vincent seems to have been an adherent of Universalism. Whether he was or not though, he went to great lengths to prove that aion and aionios are not used in the New Testament to mean eternal or everlasting and Universalists appeal to his arguments to prove their beliefs. Yet, by his own words, he admits that at times they are used in just that way. The following comments are in reference to Vincent's "additional note" on eternal destruction as found in II Thes. 1:9 (Vincent, Marvin R., Word Studies of the New Testament, Hendrickson Pub., reprint of the 2nd ed. 1888, Vol. IV, pgs. 58-62). Rightfully, he points out that these words do not, in themselves, carry the sense of "endless or everlasting." Then he points out that:

> "They may acquire that sense by their connotation, as, on the other hand, aidios, which means everlasting, has its meaning limited to a given point of time in Jude 6."

What he has admitted is that the context that words are used in is what determines their meaning. In other words, he is saying that sometimes words are used to mean eternal or everlasting, and he proves it by comparing their use with how the word aidios is used. A word, which he says, means everlasting. By showing that aidios is used of a limited time in Jude 6 while its primary meaning is everlasting, he is demonstrating that words can be, and sometimes are, used in other than their primary sense. If aidios, which means everlasting can refer to something "limited to a given point of time" then that which speaks of an age or ages certainly can be used in regard to an endless period of time as aion and aionios are in the Scriptures.

It is strange that Dr. Vincent has included this point in his over three and one-half page note on II Thessalonians 1:9 because it seems that his purpose in writing it was to

Further Considerations

prove that the "everlasting destruction" unbelievers will be punished with is only temporary. Two paragraphs later he says, "there is a word for everlasting if that idea is demanded," in reference to the word aidios. He then goes on to say:

> "That aidios occurs rarely in the New Testament and in LXX does not prove that its place was taken by aionios. It rather goes to show that less importance was attached to the bare idea of everlastingness than later theological thought has given it. Paul uses the word once, in Rom. 1:20, where he speaks of 'the everlasting power and divinity of God.'"

So, what has Dr. Vincent said here? Well, for one thing, as we shall see he has inadvertently stated that there is only one reference to God in the New Testament that demands the idea of everlastingness. What he is arguing is that if the concept of everlasting is required, the word aidios must be used. This is a word that is only used twice in the New Testament, once by Paul in Rom. 1:20 and once by Jude in Jude 6. Since its use in Jude, as Vincent acknowledges, is of a limited point in time (see previous quote), we only have one place then, according to Vincent, that the absolute idea of something being everlasting is found in the New Testament Scriptures. In his notes on I Timothy 1:16-17 in the same volume, he even implies that Paul only meant to say that God is the "King of limited ages" in his expression of praise to God for his salvation into eternal life through Jesus Christ. We wonder though, would extolling God as a "time limited" King of ages and declaring that the honor and glory due Him is only for the duration of those time-limited ages be appropriate praise for having been eternally saved by an Eternal Savior? We hardly think so (see I Tim. 1:16-17). How the translators have historically rendered this passage in our English Bibles is obviously Paul's intended meaning. And may every blood-bought saint, having believed on Jesus Christ *"to life everlasting"*, say with Paul *"Now unto the King eternal, immortal, invisible, the only wise God, be honor and glory forever and ever. Amen"* (I Tim. 1:17).

Who, having been gloriously saved by His grace from the fires of Hell and now waiting for the glorious appearing of Jesus Christ, can deny that He is the one *"Who is the blessed and only Potentate, the King of kings and Lord of lords; who only hath immortality, dwelling in the light which no man can approach unto; whom no man hath seen, nor can see: To whom be honor and power everlasting. Amen"* (I Tim. 6:15-16).

What it comes down to is that to agree with Vincent's ideas about the use of aion and aionios in the New Testament is to deny that the honor due Jesus Christ and His resurrection power are inherently eternal. We strongly object, believing that the subject matter and overall context that these verses are used in most surely demand the idea of that which is everlasting. Can the Lord Jesus Christ being revealed in the time of His glory as "the blessed and only Potentate" who is the "King of kings and Lord of lords" who alone can claim

Further Considerations

"immortality" as His rightful possession and who dwells in the "light" of glory that is beyond man's ability to see or comprehend allow for less? If there are any passages in the Bible at all that demand the idea of everlastingness, these verses must be included with them. And, contrary to Dr. Marvin Vincent's ideas, the Holy Spirit, through the Apostle Paul, used aionios here where it must mean everlasting. We can rest in the fact that Paul knew exactly what he was saying and understood its importance when he penned these words.

In his effort to do away with the Biblical teaching of eternal punishment for the wicked, Vincent also says:

> "That God lives longer than men, and lives on everlastingly, and has lived everlastingly, are no doubt great and significant facts; yet they are not dominant or the most impressive facts in God's relation to time...The relations of God to time include and imply far more than the bare fact of endless continuance. They carry with them the fact that God transcends time...."

Vincent is right in saying that God's relations to time includes more than "the bare fact of endless continuance" and that they carry with them the fact that God transcends time." However, he has missed a very important theological detail, which is the fact that it is the eternality of God's being that makes Him unique and establishes His transcendence over time and all of creation. He is terribly wrong in his assertion that the fact that God is eternal, that He has lived everlastingly and will live on everlastingly, "are not the dominant or most impressive facts in God's relation to time." The truth is that it is the fact that God is an Eternal Being who is self-existing and infinite that gives meaning to His relationship to time and everything else. Take away the concept of God's everlastingness and you nullify any idea of His absolute transcendence over creation. That He is the Eternal and Living Creator God is a dominant theme of Scripture, apart from which He would be no different than the false gods of paganism.

Vincent also claims that:

> "While aionios carries the idea of time, though not endlessness, there belongs to it also, more or less, a sense of quality. Its character is ethical rather than mathematical. The deepest significance of the life beyond time lies, not in endlessness, but in the moral quality of the aeon into which life passes. It is comparatively unimportant whether or not the rich fool, when his soul was required of him (Lk. xii.20), entered upon a state that was endless."

Here Vincent has taken it upon himself to add to the meaning of the word aionios in order to make the Scriptures fit his philosophical point of view. To say that it is relatively unimportant whether or not the rich fool (see Lk. 12:13-21) entered into a state of everlasting existence when he died is obviously ridiculous. Vincent's presupposition against endless punishment for the lost has influenced his thinking. If it makes no difference, and it is really unimportant whether life after death is endless or not, what is important? And, we can only wonder why he chose this rich man as an example instead of using the story of the rich man and Lazarus in

Further Considerations

Luke 16:19-31 where we find one man in torment and the other in bliss with an impassable gulf between them. Considering their situation, how can it be said that it makes no important difference whether one enters into an endless state of being or not after physical death? If, after almost 2,000 years, we could ask either of these rich men today what should we imagine that their answer would be? The quality of one's life after experiencing physical death is indeed important, but the duration is even more important.

Aionios is first and foremost a time word. The idea or sense of quality that is inherently associated with it is that which is conditioned by the duration of time involved. If, in reference to the life given by God, it means everlasting or eternal (see Jn. 3:15-16,36, etc.), then it most certainly can be used in the same way in reference to the judgment administered by God (see Mat. 18:8; 25:41,46; Mk. 3:20; II Thes. 1:9; Heb. 6:2).

It is interesting what Vincent says in his commentary on John 3:15 on the Apostle's use of the words zoe aionios that are translated "life eternal". He claims that it is "a characteristic phrase of John for 'live forever.'" (ibid, Vol. II. pg. 99). This is a complete contradiction of his arguments in his note on II Thessalonians 1:9 against aion and aionios being used to mean eternal or everlasting. Of course, that is not surprising because when anyone starts reinterpreting Scripture to fit their presupposed doctrine instead of reading it to see what it says, they will end up being forced into these kinds of contradictions. And that he contradicts himself in this way shows that the premise he started with is wrong, and therefore his conclusions are wrong.

THE USE OF AION AND AIONIOS IN THE SEPTUAGINT

It has been claimed by both Universalists and Annihilationists that the Septuagint version of our Old Testament cannot be used to show that the words aion and aionios were normally used to mean everlasting or eternal. Of course, they are forced into this position because if it can be shown that these words were used in the Septuagint in that way, their basic premise of only temporary punishment would be proved false and both their systems of theology would collapse on themselves. We believe that the following evidence does refute their claims.

The Septuagint is a translation of the Old Testament from Hebrew into Greek. This translation of the Hebrew Bible was done between about 280 BC and 130 BC. The Septuagint, or the LXX as it is commonly referred to in reference works, was the commonly used version of the Bible by Greek-speaking Jews during the New Testament period and by the Church in its early years. In fact, most of the quotes from the Old Testament found in the New Testament are from the Septuagint.

Further Considerations

This Greek translation of the Hebrew Bible was done to give the Greek-speaking Jews of the Diaspora (Jews living outside of Israel's Promised Land) the Word of God in their native language. It is thought that by 250 BC that there were close to a million Greek-speaking Jews living in and around Alexandria, Egypt where the translation work on the Septuagint was done.

We know that there is some question about the accuracy of parts of the Septuagint, but those problems do not negate its worth in helping to understand New Testament Greek by comparing the use of words in the two. Modern day scholars may claim that they know more about the meaning of certain Greek words than the Septuagint's translators did, but we hardly think so. What we want to remember is that this Greek translation of the Old Testament was not done by scholars far removed by time who study ancient languages, but by Hebrew scholars of the day who spoke both Hebrew and Greek from birth.

A parallel for today, to illustrate the situation, would be a man of European ancestry who was born in the U.S. but his parents emigrated from Europe. Because his family spoke their native tongue in the home and among their friends and relatives who were also immigrants, he learned that language naturally. At the same time, he learned American English as his native tongue because it was spoken in school, among his friends, and almost everywhere he went. However, when he married and began his own family, only English was spoken and his children did not learn the language of their grandparents. Later, this man wanted to pass on the rich history of his parents and their experiences in life. He took it on himself to translate the journal his father had kept and his mother's diary into English so that his ethnically European but American raised children could read them in the language they knew. The average Jew living outside of Judea did not speak Hebrew but spoke Greek. Some had been away from the land for several generations by the time that the Septuagint was done. Those who did the translating work were well versed in Hebrew as a written and spoken language and were just as proficient in Greek. Their rendering of words from Hebrew into Greek was not based on academic knowledge, historical study, and what seemed to them to be the best choice, but on a solid understanding of the two languages that they regularly read, wrote, and spoke. In general, it seems that how they used words in doing their translation is most probably how those words were normally used in their day.

AION IS USED FOR OLAM IN THE SEPTUAGINT (Which Means "Forever" or "Perpetual" In Duration of Time) to Signify Eternal or Everlasting

The following list is comprised of places in the Old Testament where either aion or aionios are used to translate Hebrew words that mean eternal or everlasting. While

Further Considerations

others may not agree that every example given is relative to the issue, we believe that there is enough evidence offered to prove that the basic premise of Universalism and Annihilationism about the use and meaning of aion and aionios is wrong and their doctrines erroneous.

> Genesis 3:22 – To eat of the Tree of Life and live forever.
>> 13:15 – The Promised Land given to Abraham's seed forever.
>>
>> 14:13 – The destruction of the pursuing Egyptian army in the Red Sea.
>
> Exodus 15:18 – The length of the Lord's reign over the earth.
>> 19:9 – How long God wanted Israel to believe Him.
>>
>> 32:13 – The duration of Israel's inheritance of the Promised Land.
>
> Deuteronomy 32:40 – The extent of God's life.
>
> II Samuel 7:13,16,24-26,29 – The time span of the house of David and his throne over God's people, Israel.
>
> I Kings 9:3,5 – God's promise to put His name in the Temple in Jerusalem forever and to establish Solomon's throne over Israel forever if he obeyed His statutes and judgments.
>
> 10:9 – God's everlasting love for Israel.
>
> II Kings 21:7 – Where God's name is to be known perpetually.
>
> II Chronicles 5:13 – the everlasting nature of God's mercy.
>> 7:3,6 – The everlasting nature of God's mercy.

7:16 – For how long God has chosen to establish His name at the Temple in Jerusalem.

9:8 – Because of His love for Israel, God has chosen to establish them forever.

13:5 – That the throne over Israel belongs to David forever.

20:7 – That the Promised Land was given to the seed of Abraham forever.

Psalm 12:7 – For how long God will preserve Israel as His people.

29:10 – The duration, past, present, and future, of God's reign as King over all.

37:28 – The length of time that the Lord preserves His saints.

41:12-13 – How long a believer is set before the face of the Lord and how long the Lord is to be praised and thanked for His goodness and mercy.

52:8-9 – For how long that man is to trust in God's mercy and to praise Him for His works.

90:2 – How long before the time of Creation God was God.

106:30-31 – The measure of the righteousness put to Phinehas' account for his being faithful to the Lord (see Num. 25:6-13).

119:89 – The length of time over which God's word is settled in heaven.

131:3 – For how long a time Israel should hope in the Lord.

Further Considerations

133:3 – The duration of the brotherhood of saints.

146:6 – The time span over which God keeps truth.

Isaiah 14:20 – How long it will be before evildoers will be renowned (or named) before the Lord.

40:8 – the everlastingness of God's Word.

45:17 – For how long the Lord will sustain Israel when He saves them. (aion and aionios are both used in this verse to denote everlastingness).

51:6-8 – The sufficiency and eternality of God, His righteousness and His salvation.

Jeremiah 20:11 – The everlasting shame and confusion God brought on Jeremiah's persecutors.

AIONIOS IS USED FOR OLAM IN THE SEPTUAGINT to Signify Eternal or Everlasting

II Samuel 23:5 – God's covenant with David.

II Chronicles 16:16-18 – God's covenant with Abraham concerning the Promised Land that was confirmed to Isaac and Jacob as an everlasting covenant.

Psalm 78:66 – The everlasting reproach put on God's enemies.

Isaiah 24:5-6 – The result of Israel breaking God's everlasting covenant.

33:14 – The everlasting burnings of the devouring fire of judgment that hypocrites fear.

45:17 – Israel's everlasting salvation by the Lord (both aion and aionios are used in this verse to denote everlasting).

Jeremiah 23:40 - The everlasting reproach and shame God will bring on false prophets (see vv. 34-40).

The State and Place of the Dead

Daniel 12:2 – Of those raised from the dead, some will have life without end and others everlasting abhorrence.

AION IS USED FOR AD AND GAD IN THE SEPTUAGINT Which Means "Perpetuity" or the "Continuance" of Time, Eternity

Exodus 15:18 – The eternality of the Lord's reign.

Psalm 9:5 – The blotting out of the names of the rebellious nations when He judges the world in righteousness (see vv. 6-8).

37:29 – In contrast to the seed of the wicked, which will be cut off from God, the righteous will dwell in the Promised Land forever (see v. 28).

45:6,17 – The perpetuity of God's throne and for how long His people will praise Him.

48:14 – For how long God will be the God of His people.

52:8 – For how long God can be trusted to be merciful.

61:8 – For how long a saint should praise God's name.

83:17 – For how long the enemies of Israel are confounded and troubled.

92:7 – the wicked may flourish briefly but will finally be destroyed forever. This is in contrast to the eternality of God (see v. 8).

104:5 – That God created the earth to last forever. (Its surface has been destroyed by a flood in the past and it will be renovated by fire in the future, but the planet earth itself will last forever).

Further Considerations

>111:3, 8,10 – God's righteousness will endure forever, His works and commandments will stand forever, and He is to be praised forever.
>
>112:3,9 – God's righteousness will stand forever.
>
>132:12-14 – The everlasting aspects of God's covenant with David and His choice of Zion (Jerusalem) as His earthly dwelling place.
>
>145:1-2 – How long saints are to praise God's holy name.
>
>148:6 – How long the creation has been established for (see vv. 1-14).

Micah 4:5 – When the Millennial Kingdom of Christ is established and Israel is exalted above the nations, His redeemed people will walk in the name of the Lord their God forever more (see vv. 1-8).

THE STATE AND PLACE OF THE DEAD

Bibliography

- Baker, Caleb J. *Life And Death*. Chicago, IL: The Bible Institute Colportage Ass'n, 1941.

- Baker, Charles F. *A Dispensational Theology*. Grand Rapids, MI: Grace Bible College Pub., 1971.

- Barnhouse, Donald Grey. *Where Are The Dead*. Philadelphia, PA: The Bible Study Hour, 1954.

- Baxter, J. Sidlow. *The Other Side of Death*. Grand Rapids, MI: Kregal Pub., 1997.

- Clark, William Edward. *The Gates Of Hades*. Springfield, MO: William Edward Clark, 1927.

- Green, Oliver B. *Where Are The Dead?* Greenville, SC: The Gospel Hour, Inc., undated.

- Gosey, C.C. *There Is No Place Like Hell*. Norfolk, VA: Clear Vision Bible Studies, undated.

- Hough, Robert Ervin. *The Christian After Death*. Chicago, IL: Moody Press, 1978.

- Lockyer, Herbert C. *Death And The Life Hereafter*. Grand Rapids, MI: Baker Book House, 1975.

- Lowry, Oscar. *Where Are The Dead?* Chicago, IL: The Bible Institute Colportage Ass'n, 1941.

- Macintosh, C.H. *Miscellaneous Writings of C.H.M.* New York, NY: Loizeaux Brothers, Vol. V., undated.

- O'Hair, J.C. *Where Is The Sould of Man' Between Death And Resurrection?*, printed Bible study. Chicago, IL: J.C. O'Hair, undated.

- Perrine, Ernest L. and Ina F. *Where Do We Go From Here?* printed Bible study. Denver, CO: Future Life Evangelistic Ass'n, 1966.

- Prince, H.B. *The Other Side Of Death*. Minneapolis, MN: The Morning Bible Hour, undated.

- Sabiers, Karl. *Where Are The Dead*. Ontario, Canada: Rex Humbard TV Minister, 1963.

- Schutz, Vernon A. *Universal Reconciliation: Do The Eons Ever End?* Grand Rapids, MI: Grace Publications Inc., 1978.

- Stam, Cornelius R. *Man, His Nature and Destiny.* Germantown, WI, Berean Bible Society, 1961:

- Thiessen, Henry C. *Lectures In Systematic Theology.* Grand Rapids, MI: William B. Eerdmans Publishing Company, revised ed. 1979.

- Vincent, Marvin R. *Word Studies of the New Testament.* Peabody, MA: Hendrickson Pub., reprint of the 2nd ed. Vol. IV, 1988.

Scripture Index

Genesis

Reference	Page
2:7	101
3:22	133
12:1-3	67
13	133
14:13	133
21:33	89
25:8	22
35:29	22
37:26-36	37
37:33	37
37:35	37
49:29,33	22
49:33	37,38
50:1-14	37
50:2-4	37
50:5-13	37

Exodus

3:6	25
12:15	96
15:18	133,136
19:9	133
31:14	96
32:13	133

Leviticus

7:20-21	96
18:21	33
19:18	18

Numbers

15:30	96
20:24,26	22
24:20,24	69
25:6-13	134
27:13	22
31:2	22

Deuteronomy

Reference	Page
4:26	109
6:4-5	18
7:9-10	69
12:5-7	57
15:7-11	17
28:1-45	14
28:44	107
30:10-20	109
30:19-20	109
32:40	133
32:48-50	22
34:5-6	26

I Samuel

28:3-20	22
28:8,11,14	40
28:15-19	40
31:1-6	40
31:7-10	40

II Samuel

7:13,16,24-26,29	133
22:13-23	22
23:5	135

I Kings

9:3,5	133
10:9	133
11:5,7,33	33

II Kings

2:11	26
16:3	33
21	133

II Chronicles

5:13	133
6:5-6	57

II Chronicles (Cont.)

Reference	Page
7:3,6	133
7:16	134
9:8	134
13:5	134
16:16-18	135
20:7	134
28:1-3	33
34:28	22

Job

Reference	Page
33:22	50

Psalms

Reference	Page
1:1-6	69
7:15	51
9:5	136
9:5,15-17	69
9:6-8	136
12:7	134
16:8-11	44
16:10	43,44,45,51
19:7	86
29:10	134
30:1-3	46
35:7	51
37:27-29	69
37:28	134,136
37:29	136
37:38-40	69
41:12-13	134
45:6,17	136
46:7	86
48:14	136
49:6-9	69
49:9	51
49:15	69
49:17-19	69
52:8	136
52:8-9	134

Psalms (Cont.)

Reference	Page
55:22-23	69
55:23	51
61:8	136
63:9-10	54
68	58
68:7-8	57
68:16	57
68:17	57
68:18	56
75:8-10	69
78	69
78:66	135
81:15	69
83:17	69,136
89:48	44,45
90:2	134
92:4-7	70
92:7	136
92:8	136
94:13	51
104:5	136
106:30-31	134
111:3,8,10	137
112:3,9	137
114:1	86
119:89	134
131:3	134
132:12-14	137
133:3	135
145:1-2	137
146:6	135
148:1-14	137
148:6	137

Proverbs

Reference	Page
10	70
10:28-30	70
11:7	70
11:29-31	70,97

Scripture Index

Proverbs (Cont.)	
Reference	Page
14:32	70
26:27	51

Ecclesiastes

1:3,9	42
2:11,17	42
9:10	42

Isaiah

1:2-5	109
9:7	94
14	48
14:4-20	38
14:6	38
14:9	38
14:10	38
14:11	39
14:12-15	39
14:18-20	39
14:20	39,135
24:5-6	135
33:14	70,135
40:8	135
40:28	89
42:5-7	15
44:23	54
45:16-17	70
45:17	135
49:5-6	15,107
49:22-23	107
51:6-8	70,135
53:10	45
56:10-12	15
60:1-3	15,107
61:5-6	107
62:1-2	107
62:1-3	15
65	96
66:22-24	70

Jeremiah

Reference	Page
17:9-10	16,93
20:11	135
23:34-40	135
23:40	135
30:3	58
33:6-8	58

Ezekiel

20:33-38	33,66
23:1-4	13
31	46,55
31:14,16,18	47,55
31:17-31	47,56
32	46,55
32:1-6	56
32:1-16	47
32:18,24	47,55
32:18,25,29	48
32:21	47
32:22	48
32:24	48
32:26	48
32:29	48
32:30	48
34:1-4	15

Daniel

2:44	94
7:13-14	94
12:1-2	70
12:2	52,67,136

Jonah

2:1-2	43
2:10	43

Micah

3:1-4	15
4:1-8	137
4:5	137

Zechariah

Reference	Page
8:20-23	15

Matthew

Reference	Page
3:7-12	96
4:11-12	66
5:22,29,30	32
5:31-32	16
6:19-21	15
7:13	96
7:13-27	96,97
7:21-23	33,66
7:23	94
8:10-12	96
8:12	32,94
10:28	32,101
12:32	85
12:40	24,45,49
13:24-30	66
13:42	32
18:8	129
18:9	32
18:34-35	95
19:3-9	16
22:1-14	96
22:23-32	24
22:32	25
22:24-40	18
23:15,33	32
24:29-31	33
24:45-51	33
25:28-30	95
25:30	32
25:30,41,46	96
25:31-32	33
25:31-46	67
25:32	94
25:34	67
25:34,41,46	97

Matthew (Cont.)

Reference	Page
25:40,45	67
25:41	32,67,68,92
25:41,46	33,94,96,129
25:46	32,89,118

Mark

Reference	Page
1:9-15	17
3:20	129
7:5-13	28
7:24-30	107
9:43,45,47	32
9:43-48	70
11:12-14	95
12:28-30	18
14:30	110

Luke

Reference	Page
1:32-33	94
1:33	86
2:11	110
4:21	110
5:26	110
9:28-36	25
12:5	32
12:13-21	128
12:16-21	28
12:20	128
12:28	110
12:36	112
13:32-33	110
16	23,50,105
16:1-13	15
16:13	15
16:14	16
16:15-16	16
16:17	16
16:18	16
16:19-31	9,14,41,42,54, 58,59,60,98,105,106,129

Scripture Index

Luke (Cont.)

Reference	Page
16:22	24
16:22-24	96
16:22-25	19,20,49
16:23-24	19
16:25	19
16:25-26	19
16:25-28	19
16:29	18
19:5,9	110
22:34	110
23:32-34	23
23:39-43	19,23,24
23:42-43	49
23:43	108,109,110
24:21	110
24:25-26	26
24:44-48	26

John

Reference	Page
1:26-34	17
3:1-36	97
3:15	129
3:15-16,36	129
3:36	96,97,115
5:25-29	52
5:27	64
5:28-29	9,45,70
5:29	64,67
8:12	15
8:12-27	97
8:21-24	97
10:17-18	44
11:1-46	23
17:3	92

Acts

Reference	Page
2:25-28	44
2:25-32	45
2:31	44

Acts (Cont.)

Reference	Page
16:30	74
16:31	74
28:30-31	114

Romans

Reference	Page
1:18-20,32	93
1:20	125
1:28-32	73
3:19	93
3:19-20,23	73
3:23-26	76
3:24	103
3:24-25	60,73
3:26	73
5:1	83,84
5:1-8:39	83
5:5	21,60
5:10-11	103
5:16-19	83
5:17	83
5:19	82,83,84
8:17-25	111
8:23	103,111
8:35-39	61,112
8:39	21
9:1-3	97
10:1	97
10:17	28
11:13	107
14:10,12	66
15:8	107
15:16	107
15:27	107
16:25-27	29
16:26	89

I Corinthians

Reference	Page
1:10-31	65
1:18	28,96,119
1:18-21	73,84
1:21	29
1:30-31	66
2:1-5	29
3:10-15	66
5:1-5	65
5:1-6:20	65
15:1-4	103,104
15:3-4	73
15:19-20	44
15:19-23	103
15:51-53	9
15:51-54	27
15:51-57	44
15:51-58	64

II Corinthians

Reference	Page
1:21-22	111
2:1-8	65
2:6-8	65
4:7	102
4:7-12	111
4:7-5:10	110
4:8	112
4:9	112
4:13-14	103
4:15-17	111
4:17	87
5:1	110
5:1-4	102,110
5:5	111
5:6-8	24,111
5:7-8	21
5:8	110
5:10	66
5:21	64

II Corinthians (Cont.)

Reference	Page
7:2-16	65
11:22-33	115
11:24-26	115
12:1-4	24
12:3-4	50
12:4	19

Galatians

Reference	Page
1:11-12	107
3:13	64
6:4-5	66

Ephesians

Reference	Page
1:6-7	65
1:7	103
1:13-14	60,73,103,111
2:1,5	60
2:4-5	102
2:8-9	102
4:7-10	53
4:8	56
4:8-9	54,55,56
4:8-10	50
4:9	46,49
4:30	111

Philippians

Reference	Page
1:12-18	113
1:19	113
1:19-26	113
120	113
1:21	113
1:21-23	20
1:22	114
1:22-23	114
1:23	112
2:9-11	93
2:10	92
3:20-21	64

Scripture Index

Colossians
Reference	Page
2:9-10	103

I Thessalonians
4:13-18	26,64,70,103
4:14	26
4:15-16	26
4:15-17	9
4:17	27
5:23	102

II Thessalonians
1:7-9	70
1:8-10	94
1:9	92,124,129

I Timothy
1:15	72
1:16	60
1:16-17	125,126
1:17	126
4:10	84
6:10	17
6:15-16	126
6:16	89

II Timothy
2:24-26	100
4:6-8	111

Titus
1:2	60
2:13-14	29
3:5	60,103
3:5-6	103

Hebrews
6:2	129
6:4-6	96
10:26	96
10:27	96

James
Reference	Page
3:6	30

I Peter
1:23	88
3:19	24
4:17-18	97

II Peter
1:4	69
1:11	94
1:13-14	102
2:4	48,67
2:12,17	96
2:17	32
3:7	96

Jude
6	67,124,125
14-15	27

Revelation
2:11	32
6:9-10	19
6:9-11	27
6:14-17	96
7:9-10,14	27
11:15	94
12:7-9	68
14:10-11	70,94
14:11	94
15:2	27
16:4-11	96
19:14-16	27
19:19-20	33
19:20	32,94
20:1-3	68
20:4-5	70
20:4-6	64,9
20:6,14	32

Revelation (Cont.)

Reference	Page
20:7-10	68,95
20:7-15	94
20:10	32,33,68,73,94
20:11-15	9
20:11-13	93
20:11-15	19,33,45,64,67,70,96
20:11-21:8	69
20:13-14	45
20:15	73,81,96
21:4	96
21:8	32,45,94,96